EXTREME
JUSTICE

EXTREME
JUSTICE

THE TRUE STORY OF THE L.A.P.D.'S SPECIAL INVESTIGATION SECTION (S.I.S.)

FRANK SACKS

A division of Shapolsky Publishers, Inc.

Extreme Justice

S.P.I. BOOKS
A division of Shapolsky Publishers, Inc.

Copyright © 1993 by Frank Sacks

ISBN 1-56171-229-9

First printing 1993.

For any additional information, contact:

S.P.I. BOOKS/Shapolsky Publishers, Inc.
136 West 22nd Street
New York, NY 10011
212/633-2022 / FAX 212/633-2123

Manufactured in the United States of America

10 9 8 7 6 5 4 3 2 1

To Paula and Spencer

CONTENTS

Part III — The Story Behind the Movie

INTRODUCTION

On Sunday, September 25, 1988, the *Los Angeles Times* broke a news story that rocked the Los Angeles Police Department and surrounding political landscape — a story that was to capture my own imagination and the next four years of my life.

In what proved to be the first exposé of its kind, the *Times* story was a remarkable profile of a once-invisible and impenetrable police unit, an ultra-secret clandestine group of detectives known among a select few as the Special Investigation Section, or "S.I.S."

Once their remarkable activities were revealed, the story was so unique that the squad's special operations attracted international attention, numerous lawsuits, a special FBI investigation, millions of dollars with which to make a movie, an exposé by Ed Bradley on *60 Minutes* and enough controversy to feed a stream of news articles that continue to be sent by satellite around the world.

The only thing more remarkable is the fact that the S.I.S. has survived all of this, and continues to operate today in Los Angeles.

The disclosure of the S.I.S. led me on a personal and sometimes precarious journey involving a stabbing, two shootings, hundreds of meetings, thousands of hours of time, millions of dollars in international financing and, ultimately, the fulfillment of a dream to make the movie — *Extreme Justice* — a film I believe you will find both powerful and controversial because it was inspired by the extraordinary activities of the S.I.S.

Today, *Extreme Justice* is being seen by a worldwide audience who are asking the same questions I believe this book will elicit from you as you judge for yourself its opinion-divisive subject matter.

While the S.I.S. continues to be encircled by conflicts, confrontations, and lawsuits, it is its volatile approach to fighting crime that gives us a rare opportunity to look firsthand at the enormous problems facing all of us as we struggle to get control of our streets.

As the story of *Extreme Justice* and the S.I.S. are an ongoing event involving more reality than fiction, we have divided this book into three parts:

Part I is "The True Story of the S.I.S." It is an investigation of the facts surrounding this secret police unit based on personal interviews and research.

Part II is the novel, **Extreme Justice**, a fictional work based on the screenplay by Frank Sacks and Robert Boris. The story was inspired by the covert activities of the Los Angeles Police Department's Special Investigation Section.

Part III is entitled **"Behind the Scenes,"** and is an insider's look at the International Independent Movie Business today. It is the story of the making of the film

Extreme Justice, and a chronicle of what happened when creativity collided with economics and power — when the story in front of the camera became totally intertwined with the action taking place behind it.

Frank Sacks
Writer/Producer

Part I

THE TRUE STORY OF THE "S.I.S."

From the first day I learned about the S.I.S., their actions struck me as unparalleled within our nation's law enforcement history. And yet, their story had remained such a closely guarded secret for nearly 23 years that the "Special Investigation Section" somehow managed to avoid both the scrutiny of an antagonistic press and recognition by Los Angeles' popular mayor, Tom Bradley—a man who for 20 years held not only the reins to one of the world's great urban centers but, coincidentally, was also a former L.A.P.D. officer.

Given those credentials, his statement that he was not aware of S.I.S. operations and their questionable mandate was remarkable. In fact, at a press conference on September 27, 1988, two days after the first story broke, he said: "The things which were disclosed were startling." What was really startling to the press was his claim to have not known about the S.I.S., as he ruled over the entire L.A.P.D. for decades.

However, today it is the unique assignments of this special unit that continue to make the real headlines, for this was and still is a group of men who are known as "The Best of the Best."

THE S.I.S.

A closer look at the profile of an average S.I.S. member proves that the aforementioned boast is not simply empty banter. Members of this elite unit average at least 15 years on the force, while their special surveillance training and experience would automatically place them at the top of any law enforcement group within the United States.

Through years of street experience, they have acquired a special ability to follow and then capture (some say ambush) some of this country's most dangerous felons. They are so incredibly adept at surveillance in particular that it has been said the FBI frequently used them to follow its own kidnapping suspects. The men of the S.I.S. are all dedicated and skilled individuals who, one detective told me, "have to have killed at least two people just to qualify to get on the unit." This one statement alone, if true, easily elevates the reputation of these highly secretive individuals to mythic proportions.

Let there be no doubt about it, today the S.I.S. continues to be a living legend within its own department. Just ask the beat cop on the streets of Los Angeles about the S.I.S. and you're likely to get a hard stare instead of information. From my experience, the regular men in blue on the streets of L.A. support this unit wholeheartedly. But the hard questions—who are they? what are they? and why have they remained protected by an invisible shield? — are questions that, when answered, only lead you to want to know more about them.

The simplest answers are to explain their way of operating and their goals — but once said, I think you will agree that the S.I.S. deserves to be placed in a very special category. Why? Because **the 19 men within the S.I.S. are assigned to identify the most dangerous and violent criminals on the streets of Los Angeles and to follow these felons, one at a time, 24 hours a day, 7 days a week — until those persons commit their next major crimes.** And, as the records would ultimately show, if you were one of those whom the S.I.S. had decided to follow . . . there was a good chance that the first time you ever met one of them, it would be the last living thing you would ever do.

Reading about their operations is to understand why their actions provoke intense debate from every side of the political spectrum, and especially from those who claim that law and order, and civil rights, can never share the same bed.

A NEW PERSPECTIVE

To look quickly at just one perspective, just imagine you're a convicted bank robber who has already spent 17 years in the State and Federal penitentiaries; that your rap sheet shows a conviction or two for second-degree murder, and that you've proven time after time you have no respect for the law and apparently have no fear of anything. You also have a never-ending drug habit and are predisposed to shooting up a mix of cocaine and heroin before you set out to rob or perhaps murder. You know that if you ever do get caught, it will lead to life in prison with absolutely no chance of parole.

Now, that's the kind of subhuman individual you and I would willingly cross the street to avoid. Right? Well, for the S.I.S. that's the kind of guy they would love to put on their little list and look forward to spending the day with.

Simply said, putting the S.I.S. on the tail of this type of criminal has proven to be the equivalent of lighting an invisible fuse to a very large and dangerous bomb. For the guilty, and sometimes the innocent, it has proven to be the fuse you just couldn't see before it blew you away.

When you consider that up to 20 men at a time have pursued this rather unusual line of work, and done so for such an extraordinarily long period of time, it is all the more strange that they managed to keep their violent activities so well hidden from the eyes of a highly critical press. How did they cover up their work for so long? Who was responsible for conceiving the entire idea? And, just exactly how do you cover up a bank shootout in which two or more people die in a wild gun battle? These can become easy answers to fill in, but there's one question that has caused the most controversy of all: What could possibly have led the S.I.S. to ultimately *watch crimes happen*?

The story of the S.I.S. is more than just one of "extreme justice." And, it is more than merely a great arena for a movie. Looking at these men and their modus operandi is a chance to examine what happens when police use near-criminal tactics to shut down the deadliest within our society. It is a philosophy that forces us to examine our own conscience about the way we enforce justice in this country. It is a story that not only encompasses the morality of the individuals involved, but also challenges every city's code of ethics, and in a greater sense asks a national question for us all to consider: Can we face the consequences of what happens when we decide to catch the criminal . . . at any cost?

Finally, it is a story that may signal the beginning of more S.I.S. units in this country. Or perhaps, it may mean the end of the Los Angeles S.I.S., the only group of its kind.

A LEVEL PLAYING FIELD

Since the first violent crime was committed, it has always been the surprise element of the perp (perpetrator) that gives him (or her) the distinct advantage. Not knowing when or where a crime will happen, coupled with the fact you simply cannot place a cop on every corner, has meant for the repeat offender, for the skilled and conniving con man, or for the serial rapist that the element of "surprise" remains the one key that inevitably leads to escape.

Apparently, someone back in the mid-sixties within the Los Angeles Police Department decided they'd finally found an answer to the game. A way to create a level playing field, so to speak, for the good guys. Simply find a crook or killer who had a high probability of repeating his line of trade, add patience, stealth, and firepower, plus a bright, dedicated group of cops, and then add that secret ingredient called "surprise" — and there was no telling what might happen. Who knows, the end result might prove very disarming or even deadly for the bad guy.

A simple theory, really. One you can't help but like . . . at first. At least, that's what we might hypothesize happened back around 1966, when the S.I.S. was formed. Unfortunately, no one is alive today who can step forward and take the credit (or blame) for the original idea. Today, the only ones stepping forward are reluctant Los Angeles City officials, nearly all of whom have denied any knowledge or control over the actions of this group they call the S.I.S. In turn, the real casualties, and the ones who did step forward to take the criticism — and the bullets — are the S.I.S. themselves, and of course the families of the dead they've left behind.

At the same time, as for the Blind Lady of Justice, the one who balances the scale of fairness in her hand, *her* decisions have shown that each side has suffered and lost major decisions in the courts.

THE BEGINNING

From what little information is publicly known, the unit apparently started out in either 1965 or 1967, depending on which source material you choose. Acting Chief of Police William Parker, together with a Detective Brown, apparently came up with the original idea of a nine-man squad of crime "witnesses": experienced policemen whose professional training would help them make mental notes as they watched a crime happen and who could make an absolutely open-and-shut case against the perps because they had the patience to wait until the crime was committed right in front of them.

With these men as witnesses, the theory was, no judge or jury would let the perps go. However, there never was, and still is, no known written policy or guideline that dictates whom the squad should follow or for how long. Nor is there apparently any written regulation about who qualifies to join or how the men are selected. When you try to get an overview, you end up wanting to compare their arrest records to the overall 7,400-man force of the L.A.P.D. And when you do, one fact in particular stands out: The men of the S.I.S. have a higher "kill ratio" than any other unit in the police department. That is, on average, each member of the S.I.S. has killed more criminals than any other ordinary policeman or unit as a whole. At the same time, only one member of the S.I.S. was ever shot by a criminal, although another stepped into the line of fire from his own men and was hit. On a less frightening level, the S.I.S. appear to arrest an average of two criminals per man year. This last statistic is about 20 percent of what the rest of the city's police do in a year; but, given S.I.S.'s rather intense approach to law enforcement, these numbers, are not that surprising.

WATCHING CRIME HAPPEN

The real crux of the first exposé about the S.I.S. touched on its intriguing secrecy. It also revealed fascinating elements of a private men's club. In fact, the S.I.S. even developed its own "cloak and dagger" insignia. (Their symbol is drawn as an outline of a man holding a dagger in one hand, wearing a black brimmed hat with a cloak drawn across his face.) A status mark, if you will, but one so secret that there are few who can appreciate its significance.

But the real shocker from the exposé was the revelation about the unit's choice of when to move in on a crime. It seems that somewhere back in time the Special Investigation Section had started crossing a line that was murky at best and yet, under numerous documented scenarios, has left quite a few people too dead to complain.

The most controversial aspect of its operations stemmed from the unit's willingness to watch criminals commit serious crimes *before* they moved in to make an arrest. In its most extreme manifestations, this became a policy that resulted in victims being beaten or threatened with death at gunpoint ... while the S.I.S. watched.

Imagine the victim's surprise or how you would feel recovering in a hospital when you learned that 19 detectives watched you get pistol-whipped but chose not to interfere because, for the criminal involved, this was a soft touch compared to the mayhem he usually inflicted upon his victims.

To think that a band of the city's elite had watched the whole thing happen from start to finish would be tough to swallow while nursing your stitches or broken bones, let alone your shattered psyche.

In one mind-boggling case in 1986, the unit followed two known criminals, Rodney Hickman and Alan Bradley, to a small retail store, called L.A. Video.

Hickman had already been identified to the police by one prior victim as the robber who had shot him, and also by three other robbery victims as the man who held them up. Hickman's accomplice, Bradley, had also been identified by two of those same victims. Yet the Special Investigation Section tracked these two dangerous ex-cons only until after they robbed the video store.

According to the store manager, Brian Ahn, the S.I.S. had watched as he and a clerk were pistol-whipped, kicked, and beaten. Only then, upon the criminals' exit, were the two perps arrested as they attempted to flee the scene—a futile attempt at that, as they were both hit by six shotgun blasts.

In court it was further disclosed that the two perps were facing more than 20 counts of armed robbery and assault, some of these charges actually pending prior to the L.A. Video robbery. Mr. Hickman got 25 years and Mr. Bradley 9 in the state prison for their work. The two employee victims in this case were lucky: they ended up alive, although they had nearly been frightened to death.

In the early days, the unit was led by Lt. Daniel Bowser, who told the *Los Angeles Times* in a brief interview that the unit was considered so elite, "We weren't even connected to a division." In other words, the men of the S.I.S. were juggled on the books from one place to another and kept wholly apart from the rest of the entire city's police infrastructure. For some reason, this initial foray into secrecy kept building upon itself in the years to come.

It was a tactic that was in direct conflict with the L.A.P.D.'s stated policy of releasing information to the public. It became a conscious effort to insure that the unit's operations (both good and bad) would never see the light of day. It is only after four years of dogged persistence by the city's most powerful newspaper that some of the S.I.S. members' identities have now been surfacing on a regular basis.

After following their activities for nearly four years, what continues to amaze me is that with 190 stories printed about them between two greater Los Angeles newspapers, and a *60 Minutes* TV exposé on them, plus all the attendant press that came with the making of the movie *Extreme Justice* ... the unit has continued to operate with near-impunity. However, the one real and major thorn in their side today is a Venice, California-based attorney, Stephen Yagman, who single-handedly pursues them with the passion of a zealot.

I met Mr. Yagman for the first time near his beach office at a dinner arranged by an intermediary. At that time, Yagman was very involved in preparing an upcoming case against the unit.

His knowledge of them has proved to be extensive.

14

Virtually all of the S.I.S. have been in front of him under oath, giving their depositions for one trial or another. He is their chief antagonist, and in a quirky bit of art imitating life wound up as an extra in the movie that was inspired by the activities of the S.I.S.

It was Yagman's first acting role in front of a movie camera and he wasn't bad, although he was quite disappointed we had written-out his favorite part: a scene in which he was to play a dead man the S.I.S. uncovers in a car trunk. (I was never quite sure how to handle that disappointment.)

As tough as Yagman has been, it always seemed odd that the most popular television show in this country, *60 Minutes*, didn't derail the unit after they ran a special segment on the S.I.S. in March of 1989. Ed Bradley's report, though viewed by more than 50 million people, never even put a dent in the S.I.S. armor. Basically, nothing happened. What also continues to surprise those who have followed the unit is the fact that a clear set of guidelines or procedures for them to follow has still not been established, or at least not revealed. Moreover, with a city approaching a siege mentality and populated by an estimated 70,000 to 100,000 gang members, you have to wonder if the problem is: Does the public really care? It is as if the Los Angeles populace is simply immune to violence. And if that's true, how can anyone blame the police if they begin to feel the same way?

Comparing the cold-blooded, nihilistic portrayal of future violence, as seen in the film *Blade Runner*, with today's headlines makes the future feel more like the present. The once remote, dehumanizing view of future violence as fiction now parallels a weekend of killing in L.A. The papers and local TV media only scratch the surface, covering just the most outlandish and violent actions. Half of those in the morgue don't even rate a two-line mention buried 30 pages into the day's stories.

Today, the voices crying out for help to fight off the criminals are not merely those of conservatives. The issue has come to affect us all. This singular point manifests itself in applause every time the S.I.S. takes out a dangerous felon in the movie *Extreme Justice*: a fact not so difficult to understand, given today's rampant and senseless daily dose of murders.

Given the above truths, trying to create an objective perspective from which to portray S.I.S. activities proved to be a formidable task. Studying the unit as portrayed by the press and making a film inspired by our research became two different things. The result was an experience that was heightened even further by our desire to obtain realistic film locations—an experience that took the cast and crew into the very bowels of Los Angeles. We went to places so dark and scary that I would challenge any reader to spend a night on the corner of 6th and Central and tell me they haven't stepped into another world.

When you experience this combat zone up close, you cross into a territory the S.I.S. has staked out as a hunting field. And you quickly discover that the humanitarian polemics of *how to deal with* this part of the world can't be debated while someone is trying to stab you.

Venturing into this part of Los Angeles is to open

up a world of philosophical territory that only the S.I.S. is prepared to deal with. What does get opened to debate is the S.I.S.'s way of conducting business in such a place. Specifically, it was their past choices to intentionally not warn a potential victim when they had received information indicating where and when a crime was due to occur. Given this same scenario, most police substitute their own men in place of the potential victims—whereas the S.I.S. has a record of, on at least four occasions, choosing not to warn anyone in advance, even though their information indicated a violent crime was going to be committed. (In our estimation, no logical explanation has emerged for this type of operation.) What has also surfaced was their bias toward watching lesser crimes happen in order to wait for the big one that would put the criminal away for a longer prison term.

Equally questionable is to consider that the S.I.S. has watched criminals move through the city knowing the criminals have an outstanding warrant from another city from a prior crime. The supposed rationale here is that busting the guy right away doesn't help solve or clear up local crimes involving the same man.

Although nearly every major metropolitan police force will from time to time set up a special unit to track highly suspect repeat offenders, only the Los Angeles Police Department has maintained such a long-standing special unit to do the job on a continuing basis. This is a phenomenon some observers have found fascinating while others have found it appalling.

THE LAST BIG MAC

By 1990, the articles in the *Los Angeles Times* were continuing to roll out on a regular basis.

It was at this time that one of the biggest stakeouts the S.I.S. ever got involved in came to light. It was an event that ultimately paralleled one scene within the movie, in that both crimes put the entire unit under intense public scrutiny. In both cases an overwhelming amount of fire power was used to stop the perps . . . while it appeared that the robbery could have been stopped before it started.

For the real S.I.S., it started with a very insignificant holdup for petty cash at a McDonald's restaurant. As the weeks went by, one after another of the fast food chain's restaurants got hit. The robbers generally waited until near closing time and then, with only a few people around, would walk in, pull their guns, and get the manager to hand over whatever cash had been put in the safe. By the time the night of February 12, 1990, came around, four teenage hotshots had nailed a total of nine different restaurants, including seven with golden arches attached. But things went wrong for everyone on that last night. And so, sometime around 2 A.M. the S.I.S. moved in and, minutes later, blasted the hell out of the perps, whose luck had fatally run out.

A few months earlier, working on a lead from another division, the S.I.S. found that the prior holdup had resulted in McDonald's management's ordering lie detector tests for several employees of a downtown franchise after it was robbed. The executives thought they recognized a pattern among the fast-food heists and there was something too close to home about this last one, which involved perfect timing by the robbers; it was definitely too smooth to be just chance. The McDonald's security people were encouraged when one employee failed the lie detector test. He was immediately fired, but nevertheless could not be arrested. Without hard evidence, admissible in court, there was no charge that could be made.

For nearly three weeks the S.I.S. followed this young man day and night. On what turned out to be his last Monday night, they watched him meet three accomplices in the Venice Beach area. The four of them drove together, in a late-model Thunderbird, to the Sunland McDonald's.

Around midnight, the four parked across the street and watched the place empty out until the only one left, at 1:30 A.M. was the manager, a young twenty-four-year-old woman named Robin Cox. At that point, three of the young men walked up to the restaurant while one stayed in the car. The S.I.S. watched as two of the perps tried to break in the back door. Ms. Cox heard them and called the police 911 hotline . . . but the police never came. They'd been told to stay clear because it was an S.I.S. operation. When the two finally broke through a side door, they were immediately joined by their friends.

Can you imagine the terror building within the young woman manager as she waited and waited for someone to come to her rescue? According to the reports, she was grabbed, tied up, and threatened at gunpoint to open the safe. She complied, and the four would-be robbers grabbed a few thousand dollars.

Months later, at the ensuing trial, some rather odd facts came out. It seems the perps had Ms. Cox on her knees at one point and in pain, until one of the young men showed a degree of compassion, helped her up, and got her a chair to sit in. At the trial there was a point made about the concern the robbers had shown for the manager's comfort.

In retrospect, all of the thieves' actions seemed amateurish and confused, but still resulted in consequences far beyond anything they thought possible.

Upon exiting the restaurant, the story totally collides with what the S.I.S. swore under oath and what the one surviving robber testified to in court. It was a situation not unlike the one portrayed in the Japanese film classic *Rashomon*. The sole survivor in this case swore his accomplices placed all their weapons in the trunk of their car upon exiting the McDonald's, and only then got in to drive off. These were weapons that all sides agreed were just pellet guns. But when the men from S.I.S. took the stand, they swore the suspects entered the car *with their guns*, and that when the unit moved in it had to block the car's escape from behind.

The S.I.S. formed a half-moon-shaped line of fire and told the perps not to move. S.I.S. testimony stated that only upon seeing two of the perps go for their guns did they blast away. Again, the story here takes two different paths, one with the surviving suspect claiming the S.I.S. unmercifully opened up on them —unprovoked. Whereas, the S.I.S. members claimed the suspects went for their guns (even though the perps were trapped, outgunned, and unable to move).

From then on, everyone agreed about one thing: that at least 35 rounds were fired from shotguns and handguns into the car in a matter of seconds, and that one individual managed to open the passenger door and flee on foot until he was brought down by more gunfire.

Later, after talking to the prosecuting attorney, he told me that an ambulance didn't show up on site for nearly a forty-minute period and that he thought it was the intention of the unit to let the fourth robber die from bleeding to death. However, he had not been able to prove this in court, and I did not pursue the matter as there were so many other elements to this particular event that were equally startling. The fact is, the Special Investigation Section's deadly way of enforcing the law was soon to become part of a much larger issue.

Soon thereafter, the surviving suspect and members of the families of those killed filed a federal lawsuit against the S.I.S., and on March 30, 1992, a jury in federal court found members of the S.I.S. guilty of violating civil rights laws and of using excessive force at the Sunland McDonald's shootout. This particular shooting also led to an ongoing investigation of the unit's actions by the FBI: an investigation that one source told me may have turned up remarkable new evidence indicating a possible conspiracy by the unit to cover up the real action that took place that night. Furthermore, an FBI spokesman has acknowledged that on Saturday, November 15, 1992, a quarter-mile stretch of Foothill Boulevard in Sunland was closed while the FBI continued its investigation of the McDonald's shootout. (Although the FBI would not directly admit it, witnesses reported that the Federal Bureau of Investigation had actually re-enacted the incident with its own men and then videotaped it.)

The events of that night also resulted in another lawsuit being filed by Ms. Cox. She claimed that the S.I.S. was negligent in its protection of her, given that they had ample cause and opportunity to move in prior to the robbery.

After it was all over, jurors in the McDonald's trial called Robin Cox a "pawn," according to a story in the *Los Angeles Times*. Another source I spoke with claimed the FBI had evidence that the guns *were*, in fact, in the trunk of the car and were subsequently planted elsewhere by the unit to make it look like self-defense — thereby giving them all an alibi for turning the crime scene into what must have looked like a film clip from the ending to *Bonnie and Clyde*. (As many will recall, this was a particularly gruesome mess, where an overwhelming burst of gunfire blew Warren Beatty and Faye Dunaway, as well as their car, into bloodied pieces of steel and bone.)

In balance, it is too easy to just believe my own source's claim of what happened, as he was not present at the time and his story is in reality still heresay, and condemning the S.I.S. without proof is anything but fair. Time will tell whether the FBI is going to step forward with any additional evidence. And, if my source is correct, a trial will surely be forthcoming. If the claims against them are proven, the S.I.S. will have a greater challenge ahead of them than any they've faced on the streets.

After having heard, as I did, the guilty verdict, you

might think the families of those left dead were somewhat satisfied with the jury's decision. However, I personally doubt this. It was obvious, from the jurors' own comments afterward, that they had mixed emotions about the whole affair. Their total awards of a paltry $44,042 in damages to the four families was less than overwhelming.

The two S.I.S. detectives fined the most—$5,005 each—were proven to have fired at least 19 of the shots between them. Seven other S.I.S. detectives were ordered to pay damages ranging from $501 to each plaintiff to $501 to only one plaintiff.

What seemed most out of balance was to learn the families' three lawyers were able to collect $387,000 in fees based on existing federal guidelines for this type of case. And, though the hierarchy of the L.A.P.D. cried out for an appeal, the City Council of Los Angeles finally decided to take a very businesslike approach to the whole matter. They paid the fines for the officers and chose not to appeal, citing the costs that would have accrued as the reason not to defend the S.I.S.

Basically, the families got next to nothing, the jury left frustrated (obviously not wanting to reward the robbers' families, or really punish the S.I.S.), and the men from the S.I.S. probably were disheartened by the verdict and angry they'd been dragged into court for doing their job. They were left with their own dead end and unable to appeal or prove their innocence because city hall chose not to back them based on the dollars it was going to cost.

BONNIE AND CLYDE FOR REAL

Nearly one year later, the S.I.S. is now due back in court again. This time from a long-standing dispute that involved two convicted bank-robbing felons, one male and one female, and their child, who at that time was a three-month-old fetus. In 1982 the expectant parents had the misfortune of being put on the S.I.S. agenda.

The father was Johnny Crumpton, thirty-three years old. The mother-to-be was Jane Berry, thirty-six. Both were parolees who had been tied to five bank robberies. In addition, they were actually wanted on outstanding federal arrest warrants when the S.I.S. decided to start tailing them day and night. By the time the first part of this case rolled into Federal Court, in early June of 1990, I had already written a dozen different drafts of a screenplay about the S.I.S. and was beginning to get the feeling I was never going to get down on paper the right approach to their story.

Once again, now two years into my own fascination with the unit, another chance to do more research came up. This time I decided to go see for myself what these guys looked like in person. Up until then, I had avoided all third-party offers to meet them; but now they were coming to trial for an event that had taken place nearly eight years earlier. And, although I still had mixed emotions about sitting in a federal courtroom surrounded by men whose secret professional lives I had decided to try and make into a movie, I got in my car and drove downtown to the Federal Court Building.

I spent parts of two different days in that courtroom listening to their testimony and to the lawyers on both sides, butting heads over technical issues that at times appeared to bring the whole process to a slow, boring crawl. What kept this heartbeat going, though, was seeing in person for the first and only time the men of the S.I.S.

As there were few spectators, I would occasionally catch one of them looking my way, possibly wondering what had brought me to watch their trial. They were all grouped together on one side, sitting in three or four rows of hard-backed wooden pews. Several women were present with them at various times, and I wondered who they were? Possibly girlfriends and supportive wives? There seemed to be a lot more tension on the spectator side than on the other, where the judge, jury, and lawyers sat. Occasionally, the S.I.S. would whisper among themselves, and every once in a while one of their beepers would go off and you'd see one of them leave the room.

I wondered whether other S.I.S. members not present were reporting in from a stakeout in progress? And once, when I came back after lunch before they did, two of them sat beside me on what I now considered *my* side of the courtroom. I distinctly remember the one to my right crossing his legs, which exposed a small revolver strapped to his ankle. I was nervous. Actually, I think we were all nervous. In front of us the trial moved on, but my own attention kept coming back to the female bank robber sitting less than ten feet away.

(There's something quite strange about a woman

who robs banks. It just doesn't go together. Perfume and bullets? Coiffed hair and heroin? I guess I still hold a male prejudice against equal rights for women when it comes to robbing banks. I simply see it as a male's domain.)

As this trial marked the first time the entire S.I.S. group was being called into question, there were evidently some very serious repercussions for all those involved, if found guilty.

Ms. Berry's lawyer contended (again, he was Stephen Yagman) that his client's civil rights had been violated under federal law; he was asking the jury for $10 million dollars in damages. His case aimed at pointing out to the jury that Ms. Berry's now-deceased boyfriend, Johnny Crumpton, had been murdered—by what Mr. Yagman not so politely referred to as a "death squad." The federal judge was less than thrilled with his choice of words and ordered Mr. Yagman not to call them a "death squad" again.

S.I.S. surveillance of the couple had begun July 26, 1982. Each was wanted on federal warrants for violating parole. (The two S.I.S. members who supervised their 18-day surveillance swore in court that they had never run a current check on the suspects and were unaware of the outstanding warrants.) However, later it was revealed that another member of the S.I.S. was aware that on one occasion Mr. Crumpton had mercilessly shot a robbery victim in the back as he lay facedown on the floor.

Crumpton and Berry were pretty "wired" on the day they decided to hit the Bank of America; both had shot up a mix of cocaine and heroin. The S.I.S. was on their tail starting that morning, from the moment they left their Silver Lake motel. The two bank robbers drove separate stolen cars to the bank, and passed by it several times before parking. They decided to leave one of the cars at a nearby location and together drove the other car back to the bank. Once they'd parked, they donned bizarre wigs, Halloween masks, and rubber gloves before going in—all in sight of one S.I.S. member.

Later, when Ed Bradley interviewed Ms. Berry on *60 Minutes*, he asked her what she would have done if someone had made a wrong move (in the bank). She said, "I probably would have . . . destroyed everything that moved." Statistics from the Department of Justice show that one out of every three robberies ends with a victim getting injured (supporting Ms. Berry's potential to be violent). The point Bradley was trying to make was that if anything had gone wrong in the bank and someone had been hurt, it would have been a calculated risk the S.I.S. should not have taken. To some, it appears the S.I.S. simply chose to watch them getting ready prior to entering the bank and in a premeditated fashion chose not to intercede.

60 Minutes also asked the then-Acting Chief of Police, Daryl Gates, why the S.I.S. didn't arrest them at that point? He said, "They couldn't, I'm sure. Actually I shouldn't say that. I'm not sure they were close enough to move in at that point. I think there was probably a distance problem. They could have grabbed them, but if you think that is enough to get a conviction for anything, you're foolish. . . . It is not." As the segment went on to prove, others in authority disagreed entirely with Chief Gates's opinion. (Within one more year, there were so many people in Los Angeles fed up with the Chief's overall actions and opinions that he was pressured into retiring early.)

The CBS show also recited in particular the California law concerning "conspiracy to commit robbery," which has a penalty equal in punishment to actually committing the crime. In other words, if they'd been stopped before they entered the bank, they could have probably been sentenced to the same jail terms.

For me, listening to the live court testimony and glancing at the blonde bank robber in front of me seemed incongruous—especially after she revealed alarming testimony about questionable S.I.S. behavior: She claimed that she and her accomplice left the scene of the robbery with no problem but were attacked when they attempted to switch getaway cars at a nearby location. She later recalled for *60 Minutes* what she had remembered when the shooting started. She said: "Just shooting . . . continual shooting, and I remembered . . . like in seconds you don't know you're being hit, but uh . . . I was hurt because I was bleeding out of my mouth already."

She was definitely hurt alright—but nothing like her lover, Johnny, as four of the S.I.S. were well positioned to fire upon him. Testimony from one of the S.I.S. men claimed they opened fire when they thought she was reaching for her weapon. And though her boyfriend was unarmed, and, she claimed, she never went for her gun (she was three months pregnant at the time), they were both struck by a barrage of shotgun blasts.

Eighteen shotgun shells later, Johnny had been hit only from behind and had 32 holes in his legs and 23 in his shirt. The autopsy report showed he even had bullets that had entered through the bottom of his left foot! Their lawyer at the time said that the S.I.S. *executed* John Crumpton and that he (the lawyer) was sure the penalty for robbing a bank in this country was not death. Either way, it was definitely Johnny's last bank robbery.

One other note: One month earlier these two had actually robbed the same bank, wearing the same masks, guns in hand.

Given the above, most people either take the position (1) that the S.I.S. should be thanked for taking these two off the streets or (2) that they were wrong to wait until after the crime was committed, and should have busted them before it all came down. Those with the latter opinion, after looking at drawings that show an inordinate number of shots in Johnny's back, question whether the unit had simply set them up like clay pigeons.

Apparently the jury was not so confused about what to think: The outcome of the trial was a "Not guilty" verdict for the S.I.S and the civil rights case against them was dismissed.

Today, one of the more bizarre footnotes to this episode is the newly filed case on behalf of Ms. Berry's then-unborn child. The boy is now nine years old. One "high" court has already ruled that his civil rights were possibly violated, (while in the womb), as his father died in a robbery that perhaps should have been stopped before he and the boy's mother entered the bank. (Editor's note: The trial is scheduled to begin in Los Angeles as this book goes to press.)

Once you become aware of some actual S.I.S. cases it becomes clear why there is a real problem in trying to get a perspective that rings true for this group. The question is: Can you really judge any of the S.I.S. without having actually participated in the shootings? And, are the questions of when to move in and how much force should be used always going to be just a matter of opinion?

WE GET LETTERS

On August 27, 1991, I was suddenly made aware of what proved to be a very "special" opinion. That was the day I received a four-page letter from a member of the S.I.S. Herein, I quote directly from it:

Having read *Variety* dated 7/25/91 about your upcoming movie, "S.I.S." [editor's note: retitled *Extreme Justice*], I felt I must write to you about my concerns about your statements "We are not trying to denigrate the police or what they do. It's an extremely controversial film that cannot help but raise questions surrounding the legal, ethical and moral issues of a police force using such questionable tactics in apprehending criminals."

Having read the script of your movie six or so months ago, I would say the way it's written (scenes) does raise questions.

I hope that I've remembered things correctly about the script. Having knowledge of S.I.S. and how it operates, I wonder about your sources. If the two newspaper articles at the beginning of the script and other newspaper articles are some of your sources, I realize your information is lacking.

If some of this information has come from police officers or attorneys, they have flowered it up for unknown reasons. They don't have the knowledge of how the unit really operates. If you are going by the numerous articles in various newspapers, most of them are very one-sided. Some of the articles express the one-sided views of the criminals' attorney. Some of the views are views of the person or persons who are writing the articles for headline-grabbing journalism. Reading the script, I get the following impressions of some of the people and scenes.

(The S.I.S. member then describes five of the scenes from that particular draft of the script—all of which were ultimately changed, but were inspired by true events.)

The writer went on to say:

I believe these scenes show S.I.S. in a derogatory manner to the public and to the family members of S.I.S. officers. None of the scenes are truthful. You mention tactics used by S.I.S. in your statements. We train many, many hours in reference to tactics. The fact is that we do not set up inside banks in an attempt to arrest suspects as they are committing the robbery. The reason is very simple: to prevent a hostage-type occurrence and a shootout, as described in your script. The *Los Angeles Times* newspaper articles by David Freed refer to S.I.S. as a secret unit. The word "secret," I believe, means "done, made or conducted without the knowledge of others." There were a lot of people who knew about S.I.S. prior to his articles in the *Los Angeles Times*. Officers testified in open court on cases. So judges, defendants, attorneys, and people sitting in court were aware. Newspaper articles about arrests and the news media attending a funeral of an S.I.S. member killed in the line of duty in 1980 also made people aware. The funeral was covered by the *Los Angeles Times*. City officials attended the funeral along with Mayor Bradley or his representative.

Mayor Bradley shortly thereafter obtained information from an S.I.S. member about body armor for himself. I guess just because David Freed doesn't read his own paper or didn't know, that makes it a secret. But I guess a lot of people don't know things, and that makes those things a secret.

I failed to read anything in your script about all the hours S.I.S. officers have spent in dangerous situations such as covering kidnaps for ransom money drops. Finding an eight-year-old kidnap victim taped and blindfolded [after] being held for two days in the back seat of a car. Acting as go-betweens in money drops and being exposed to being shot or kidnapped themselves. Finding a six-year-old kidnap victim alone in an apartment after suspect attempted to run down officers during a money exchange. The numerous other kidnap victims recovered unharmed, due to the actions of S.I.S. officers. The arrests of multiple robbery suspects who were armed and taken into custody without incident.

Other suspects [taken] such as the Freeway Strangler (William Bonin), the Hillside Strangler, the Alphabet Bomber, etc.

I guess my main concern is that the script shows a distorted view of S.I.S. and its officers, as do numerous news articles and statements from some attorneys. The script is one-sided and indicates a unit that is out of control and is only into killing suspects. I realize that when you make a movie it's got to be exciting and action-packed, but how about truthful facts? Thanks for taking time to read about all my concerns.

Maybe the next movie, with better facts, could be called "S.I.S.: The Real Story."

In retrospect, the above letter seems level-headed and certainly not the writing of a "fascist" or some guy on a "death squad." And, though I could make counter-points and criticize his letter, it is the *issues* involved that deserve the real debate and not just one S.I.S. operation or our filmmakers approach to bringing the issues to the public's attention. The question of how to combat the country's most violent and dangerous criminals has obviously not led either the S.I.S. or the general public to an easy answer.

However, at the time I received the letter, it upset me and my wife. A hard-news writer or professional crime reporter would be immune to involving himself with such a volatile group . . . I was not. At times, I have been worried, perhaps fearful about what might happen to me from making a movie inspired by the S.I.S. Many friends have, in fact, asked me if I was worried? Worried about what? has been my only answer.

I've considered that 100,000 films and TV shows have been made about the police, the CIA, the FBI, and the L.A.P.D. — without repercussion. But to do a film about the perhaps most interesting law enforcement unit in the country has actually been a frightening experience now and again.

Tackling a group like the S.I.S. is not like writing something for Walt Disney. Therefore, given the subject matter, I've accepted that a certain degree of fear was a natural reaction. What really bothered me at the time I received the S.I.S. letter was that a script I had kept under wraps had ended up being reviewed by the S.I.S. itself. (I still don't have a clue about which friend or associate passed it on and apparently had an acquaintance who was or knew an S.I.S. member.)

Although the letter was more of a critique, and I saw nothing within it as a personal threat to me or my family, I was not inclined to respond by calling this S.I.S. member, even though he had given his address and two phone numbers beneath his signature.

One fear I had was that getting to know one of the S.I.S. would unduly influence my perspective on writing *Extreme Justice* What if I became intimidated by a less-than-positive chat with one or two of them over a drink? Or became too sympathetic to their position? In either case, whatever objectivity I still had would have gone up in smoke.

All of the foregoing has forced me to look as closely as possible at that word, "objectivity." It has become a real nemesis in trying to evaluate the S.I.S. In turn, moving toward the release of a movie without knowing what its ultimate effects might be has been unsettling. There is no guaranteed method of gauging how a movie audience will react. What if the film became a catalyst for putting the S.I.S. out of business? Or, had the opposite effect—and made them into worldwide heros? During the time I have debated about how to treat the subject matter, I have also continued to have personal experiences that made me thank God we have a Los Angeles Police Department. One example:

At 11 P.M. on January 10, 1992, while sitting at home reading what must have been the twenty-fifth draft of the script, I heard three distinct backfires of a car blocks away. Thirty seconds later, screeching tires around the nearby corner really caught my attention, and before I could get up from my desk I heard a series of fast-braking cars. Moving twenty feet to the front window, I cautiously peered through a break in the curtains and saw what looked like the entire L.A.P.D. running with shotguns in hand to position themselves directly across the street from my front window. In unison they trained their guns on me.

Without needing to think, I dropped to the floor and started crawling toward the back bedroom. Upon meeting my wife halfway there, also on her knees, we forgot all else except our baby, and together looked out the back window at our yard—which was lit by a helicopter beacon. (It reminded me of *Close Encounters of the Third Kind*, the part where a million-kilowatt ray lit up the ground.)

Single file, we crawled on all fours back to the front of the house, passing our infant's bedroom but deciding to let him sleep. With the phone in hand I dialed the emergency number, "911." To my dismay, the operator answered by saying: "You live at . . ." (She gave our exact address.) "We have located armed and dangerous robbers in your backyard. Keep the lights off, stay down and don't move!"

Over the next two hours, the L.A.P.D. cordoned off the block, moved in, and located the three jerks who'd climbed up the backyard avocado tree. The perps had robbed a patron at a nearby 7-11 store who turned out to be an off-duty cop. The ensuing gun battle somehow ended up in our backyard. Ultimately, they tree'd these idiots and took them away. The L.A.P.D. had proven to be not just a luxury but a necessity. The point acknowledged, was I making a movie that would harm the very entity I needed to help protect my family's well-being?

The same question would reoccur to me again several times during the course of making the movie — in much more dangerous situations. But those are events placed at the end of this book in the section entitled "Behind the Scenes."

Another attempt to retain "objectivity" and fairly judge the S.I.S. actions involved my reading the research of *one particular Los Angeles Times reporter*, the same reporter who was referred to in the letter I had received from the S.I.S. member: David Freed. Freed's in-depth research was at the heart of the *Times*'s investigation series and, when combined with Stephen Yagman's court room evidence, was the bible for what we know today about the performance of the Special Investigation Section.

As a staff reporter, Freed's lead article in true *Los Angeles Times* style was thousands of words long and covered research involving 32 S.I.S. cases in which at least one perp was shot. As he stated, "... more than 200 police officers, crime victims, witnesses, criminals, prosecutors and defense attorneys were interviewed." His work was, quite simply, a remarkable assemblage of crime facts and conclusions that appeared in his first and succeeding stories.

Freed's point of view could not be hidden, unfortunately, even though you had the feeling he was trying to be objective. What emerged (despite his efforts?) was a conclusionary style and disposition that would leave even the conservative law-and-order types asking whether or not the S.I.S. had finally reached its time to retire. Freed's statistics and his conclusions seemed both rational and tempered, and yet I for one have doubts about any such necessity because no one from the S.I.S. will—or can?—get into any lengthy debates.

Overall, Freed cited numerous city and federal officials who support his contention that the S.I.S. has crossed over to a point of no return. And though my own research pales in comparison to his, I have ultimately felt in my gut that his analysis is not as black-and-white as he's logically portrayed it to be. Coupled with my own agenda is my belief the *Los Angeles Times* is in the business of selling newspapers. And, though I may be accused of being cynical, I believe that too many reporters in the '90s—whether their trade is the written word, TV, or radio—are increasingly influenced, if not harassed, by the bottom line. It is sales and ratings that also shape the thinking of those who serve the fourth estate. The competition among them to seek the largest audiences and the lowest common denominator gives us page-one items and lead stories on the evening news that were once only found in the cheapest supermarket tabloids. From my perspective, there are no longer any Edward R. Murrows, and it is very difficult to find totally balanced and truthful reporting today.

Adding in my own research and the events that have affected me directly during the four years I've devoted to this endeavor, I conclude that there *is* a need for an S.I.S., but that, like all those who serve the people, it too must be closely watched.

To some, this opinion may seem like a merciless point of view, considering the level of violent engagements that are a part of the S.I.S. record. And, there is no question that the S.I.S. way of conducting business certainly goes against Judeo/Christian beliefs of "turning the other cheek." However, today is an especially difficult time for those who are sworn to try to keep the streets safe. And, although we can philosophize all day long about *how to fight crime*, the fact is, if you've ever had a gun put to your head, if you've ever been robbed, if you've ever had your security violated, it becomes exceedingly difficult to talk philosophy and not wish to react or have someone do it for you—perhaps violently! Becoming violent when facing down a gun when your life is at risk is normal. What is abnormal is the rising degree of probability that that "someone" will be you.

The character of "Kelly Daniels," as a reporter within the film *Extreme Justice*, expresses my own feelings about the S.I.S. best when she says, "No one individual has the right to be judge, jury, and executioner in our society."

Nevertheless, if *we* are going to judge the *S.I.S.*, we should be prepared to judge ourselves, too, because we are ultimately responsible for what happens on our streets. However, if you are among those who find it impossible to accept the S.I.S.—on any terms—at least accept the opportunity to confront the issues the S.I.S. has forced us all to face. Regardless of your own conclusions about *how*, we should handle the most dangerous of our species, at least you will be among those who care enough to think about it.

What now follows is the novel based on the screenplay of *Extreme Justice* . . . .

Part II

EXTREME JUSTICE

Tyrone Deacon could feel the rush through his arm, and then an explosion of light behind his eyelids. The mix of heroin and cocaine hit his heart and brain at the same time. It was enough to make a smaller man pass out, but Tyrone could take the pressure, the rush that made him forget it all.

As his eyes rolled back, he heard the pounding of his heart, and his mind soared, pushing through hallucinatory white clouds--higher and higher. His hands trembled as the cocaine took hold. He unconsciously let the needle slip from his fingers and dangle loose in his forearm. He loved it. He loved it all.

Still hidden in the shadows of a dark alley near 6th and Central, he rocked back against a red brick wall. He was only a mile from the business center of the city, just a few blocks south of downtown L.A., but it might as well have been another world . . . and it *was*.

When the heroin made him break out in a sweat, he didn't care. Tyrone could take the heat. He was ready to step out and take care of business.

He was in a world apart, and neither the stench of urine or stale garbage all around bothered him in the least. Ahead of him lay the street, with just enough light filtering his way to see the bullet in the chamber when he cocked the .45 in his hand. He felt no pain and didn't notice the needle when it finally slipped out of his arm and fell to the ground.

Tyrone stopped just before exiting from the alley when he suddenly felt something strange, as if someone was watching him.

He was high, God he was so high, but he knew himself well enough to pause for a just a moment . . . just to be sure he was safe. He cautiously looked both ways up and down the deserted street and watched a bum push a rusty grocery cart down the sidewalk. The old man didn't even look his way; he'd given up looking at anything a long time ago.

To his left, thirty feet away, another bum wearing a filthy raincoat could barely stand. This guy was holding tight onto the light post to keep from falling facedown into the gutter. The bum's body wrenched from the effects of a bottle of cheap wine.

As the high settled in, Tyrone could feel the juice pumping through his big frame. He was big, all right, as there was nothing to do in the slammer but lift weights, all day, every day, as he'd done for twelve of his last fifteen years in prison. It was time he'd spent for multiple armed robberies and an added term for stabbing another inmate. *A real idiot, that guy*, thought Tyrone. He'd believed Tyrone was one of the boys and had tried to bugger him in the shower.

As he walked past the wino in the dirty raincoat, Tyrone thought he saw him glance his way. No matter, it was no concern of his.

Ty was cool now and it was time to take care of business. He walked past a flea-bag hotel and headed for the corner liquor store. It was nearly eleven P.M. and he knew the till would be full up. It was the second Friday of the month, payday. The day every wino in the neighborhood had gotten his welfare check.

Behind him, the drunk suddenly managed to stand tall. He watched Tyrone with such intense concentration it betrayed his ragged clothes and made it obvious he knew who Tyrone was and what he was all about. Detective Dan Vaughn raised the empty wine bottle in his hand to cover his mouth and whispered into a concealed mic on the inside of his sleeve: "This is the quarterback. The ball is in play."

As Tyrone neared Tiny's Korean Liquor store, his adrenaline kicked in and gave him another boost. He was on a roll now and he knew it. He'd knocked over five other skid-row joints like this in as many weeks. He knew the clerks always had a piece, but he also knew if you walked in hard and put the .45 right in the motherfuckers' face, they near pissed in their pants and forgot all about trying to get the drop on you. Nobody got the best of Tyrone, nobody.

Down the street, two unmarked cars slowly turned the corner and rolled to a silent stop. In the first, Ian Cusack sat behind the wheel: forty-seven years old, blond hair, a bull dog in plainclothes, and at six-two, two forty-five, this second-generation Polack was feeling that tonight would be Tyrone's last. His partner, an even larger, black man, named Larson, picked up the mic and calmly responded, "The team is on the field, we're almost there."

Larson put the mic down and loaded three more high-density shotgun slugs into the Remington.

Larson was another character to watch operate. For that matter, all three were characters in one way or another. But Larson's thing was cowboy clothes. He had the whole rig: boots, hat, and duster—but at six-foot-five and two hundred-eighty pounds, nobody had ever told him they didn't like his outfit.

Closely following their car were Webber and Reese: both mid-thirties, with nothing quite so distinguishing on as Larson, except the concentration on their faces. Each held within himself the same controlled sense of confidence, of the inevitable, that was about to take place.

They drove slowly by Tiny's. Webber stopped his car halfway down the street. He unholstered his automatic and re-checked the clip. Somehow, he also knew this time they'd nail him and that they wouldn't have to let Tyrone Deacon go again. Webber watched through binoculars as Tyrone pulled a pair of dark glasses from his pocket and stopped at the open door into Tiny's. He nervously glanced up and down the street one last time. There were no black-and-whites in sight.

Tyrone walked into Tiny's and pulled the big .45 from under his jacket. He boldly raised the gun and aimed first at the unlucky clerk behind the counter and then at the two customers. Hearing his menacing tone, none of them mistook his willingness to shoot.

"Don't move, motherfucker!" He turned on the customers, "You two, down on the floor, NOW! I swear I'll kill both of you, I said MOVE!" The two patrons dropped facedown onto the floor, the clerk moved back a foot, but before he could say anything Tyrone hopped the counter and in one swipe broke the Korean's nose with the steel butt end of his gun. The clerk's head bounced off the glass behind them. It shattered into a hundred pieces.

Tyrone moved quickly to the cash register and had it open in seconds--but it was empty. This made him mad and, worse yet, he was starting to come down off the drugs. "Where is it? Where's the damn cash, man? I mean it . . . !"

The clerk felt warm urine running down his pants leg. His heart beat so hard he thought it would burst. He'd just put fifteen hundred in the safe. He was scared to death, he pointed to the safe below the register and tried to speak. "I no have key. Money in safe. Please, please don't kill me."

Tyrone didn't like Orientals, and answered him by viciously pistol-whipping him again and again.

On the street, Detective Vaughn could hear Tyrone yelling and the Korean pleading for his life, but he didn't move in. It was coming down, this was the night. Vaughn pulled a .50 caliber Israeli Desert Eagle from the holster under his arm and calmly spoke into a hidden mic, "O.K., he's in. Get set. It's real."

Across the street, four Detectives moved as one unit, crossing to his side and bracing themselves be-

47

hind the parked cars near the store entrance.

Another Detective dressed as a wino suddenly appeared from around the corner. Angel's bearded Cuban face, dark eyes, and greased hair made him a perfect fit for this neighborhood. He concealed his own gun within a brown paper bag and used the lamppost on the corner to steady his aim on the empty doorway. Between Angel and Vaughn they'd have Tyrone in a crossfire, and their four partners backing them with shotguns and automatics aimed the same way.

Tyrone listened to the Korean plead. He hated this whimpering sonofabitch more than the fact he'd only pulled a lousy twenty bucks out of the cash register. At point-blank range, Tyrone squeezed three rounds into the Korean. One of them went through his right eye and exploded out the back of his head. "Fuck you, you little shit!" were Tyrone's parting words to the dead store owner.

He turned on the two customers cowering on the floor, but decided not to waste the ammunition. Slowly he backed out of Tiny's.

Vaughn stood less than twenty feet away as Tyrone came out with his back still to the street. Tyrone suddenly turned when he heard Vaughn call his name. "TYRONE!" Someone else said, "Drop it!" But Tyrone was too stoned to really understand. And then it was too late. The first five rounds entered his chest and neck. Two shotgun blasts opened his stomach; another took his left hand completely off. Reflexively, Tyrone managed to get one shot fired and it ricocheted off the sidewalk and hit Detective Reese in the knee cap. The cop fell to the street screaming in pain. Larson looked down at his bloodied friend and opened up. Two more shotgun blasts lifted Tyrone off his feet. His dark glasses were blown away from his face, exposing just the whites of his eyes. Three more rounds slammed through the center of his heart.

Tyrone was already dead but the impact of so much firepower kept him propped up against the doorway until the shooting stopped, and then he just slid straight down into a pool of his own blood. A nod from Vaughn to the rest of his men was all it took to know it was over. It was time to call in the regular L.A.P.D. and let them clean up the mess. It was time to go have a drink with the boys.

THE CODE SEVEN BAR

In every town or city there's at least one cop bar: a place where the guys can hang out, get fucked up, and say what they want without worrying about who might overhear. When you're surrounded by your own kind, it feels right; and with the Code Seven Bar just a block from City Hall, it had been a fixture for nearly two decades for the men of the S.I.S. It didn't matter to the guys inside that it was smoky and dingy, or that some thought it was a dump: It was theirs.

For Vaughn's men, it was a place to go. A place where they could be together after an event like the shootout at Tiny's. A place to talk among themselves about how the perp had been dead for a good twenty seconds before he even dropped to the ground ... about how the Korean had the back half of his head splattered all over the floor ... about how Larson's double hit had lifted the fucker clear up on his toes before he dropped. It was the kind of talk that had to be said before they went home to their girlfriends, their wives, and their kids. And though they were all professionals and each of them had killed before, none of them, except Vaughn, was immune to the consequences. In a twisted way, it was like a post-game party where you were still so pumped up you needed to keep talking about the highlights — except in this case it was the bullet count. A psychologist would say it was normal behavior, but to anyone on the outside the conversation would have seemed sick, even macabre. Still, that's the way it was and also why very few outsiders were ever allowed to spend time in the Code Seven. And so they drank their beers, their whiskey, and they played poker for quarters through the rest of the night until they'd chilled out and Cusack brought up the one subject no one wanted to discuss: Reese.

Cusack got the ball rolling when he asked Vaughn, "What are we gonna do about Reese? His knee was pretty fucked up."

Vaughn knew exactly what he was going to do, but kept quiet until the rest of them had spoken, and then he said, "Reese was good, all right. At least he didn't go home in a box."

A long silence passed as they drank up and traded looks that said a lot more. They all knew it could have been them. One random slug and any one of them was an instant desk jockey, for life.

Larson wondered aloud, "Where we gonna find another guy like Reese?"

Vaughn thought he'd never ask. "I've got someone in mind."

It was the look in Vaughn's eyes that convinced Angel right then and there that they were in for a little surprise. He knew Vaughn loved games. He also knew Vaughn always played for keeps.

THE NEW MAN

Jeff Powers had learned to drive when he was only thirteen. He was behind the wheel of a stolen car and totaled the Cadillac, barely escaping over a wall when the cop chasing him was too fat to scale it. Powers was lucky: he was one of just a few home boys in his barrio neighborhood who had not done time by his eighteenth birthday. It was a neighborhood where one out of ten would be shot by gang bangers. Where one out of fifteen would be shot dead before he had reached his twenty-first birthday.

Somehow, his smile, his sense of humor, and certainly his good looks had gotten him a lot farther than most. In school, the girls passed their answers to him, hoping he'd ask them for a date, while the teachers saw a raw spark in his eyes and a quickness to his mind that others in his class would never possess. He managed to graduate and stay out of harm's way. He was lucky, no doubt about it.

That is, until the day his dad was shot dead by a vagrant. Just another bum in the neighborhood. But this one had gone over the edge and pulled a gun when his father caught him breaking into their house. Jeff heard the gunshots. He was down the block hangin' on the corner with his friends. He knew the sounds were too close to home and ran as fast as he could to get there. His father was already dead when he ran in the front door and found him on the living-room floor.

Jeff's rage and anger overcame any sense of caution. He knew the killer could not be far away. He ran out the open back door and looked down the alley, where he saw the vagrant just walking away still holding the gun in his hand. Jeff heard sirens in the background as he started toward the man, but before he could get close enough the guy turned on him and fired.

Jeff felt the bullet whistle by his head but it wasn't going to stop him. He moved toward the killer again and would have been a statistic if a cop hadn't shot the guy.

But the killer was only wounded. He turned and fired at the cop, hitting him in the arm. The officer spun in pain from the bullet, then took aim again and this time shot the sonofabitch dead. Jeff studied this man he had never seen before; a guy he didn't even know but who saved his life.

The look on the cop's face was one of confidence and pride, a look that made Jeff Powers realize in the years to come that he had discovered a path to follow, a way to be the avenger and not just another victim.

In the city's police academy he had graduated near the top of his class and, at first, it looked as if he was going to be a regular in the L.A.P.D. And then, things just sort of went back to the way they were. The streets made him tougher, impulsive, and a little too reckless— traits a regular cop didn't want in a partner. Powers had a reputation for a short fuse and would just as soon fight as arrest the hood he had caught.

He possessed the kind of edge that earned respect from those on the streets but continued to get him on

Frank Sacks

the Sarge's list. It was the kind of edge Dan Vaughn
understood.

A LITTLE REVENGE

Jeff Powers knew that if he had one more screw-up, he was off the force, but he had decided long ago that losing his badge to collar Eddie Payton would be worth it. Powers had had a tip that Payton had gotten out on bail that afternoon. He also knew Payton to be the lowest kind of scum there was: a child molester. Once before when Jeff Powers finally had a chance, he had staked out Payton on his own and almost caught him sodomizing a ten-year-old girl. It was the third time Eddie Payton had struck, and should have been the last time Payton was allowed on the streets, but a technicality had forced the judge to let him loose again.

Now, Powers had finally decided that no matter what he had to do, he wouldn't be letting Eddie Payton get away.

Jeff had waited eleven hours in his car with his partner, Art Blake. Finally, they saw Payton pull up to park in front of his apartment. When Payton looked up and saw who was waiting for him across the street, he didn't hesitate to gun the engine and tear away.

Jeff made a sharp U-turn and sent Blake careening off the window. "What the hell are you doin', Jeff?"

"I'm not losing this creep again," answered Powers.

Blake had been with Powers long enough to know he was in for a rough ride. He tried to be sensible. "Dammit, Powers! I'm calling for backup."

Jeff yanked the mic out of Blake's hand. "Fuck the

backup, I'm breaking a restraining order just chasing the guy."

Blake's eyes widened as they hit the first stop sign and barreled right through it. He had to have an answer. "Then, what the hell are we doing?!"

Powers pressed the accelerator a little more and smiled. "We're getting the job done..." With that, Jeff slammed into the back of a pickup truck. "Oh, shit," he said, and threw the gears in reverse, wheeled out, and resumed his high-speed pursuit.

Two hundred yards in front of them Eddie Payton looked in his rearview mirror and saw Powers gaining. Eddie was a frightened little man and knew it was all over if he let Powers catch him again. He skidded out of control on his next turn and found himself racing down the median line of the busiest street in east L.A.

Cars on both sides came within inches of his sedan, but he didn't care. But for that matter, neither did Powers since he was driving on pure hate and adrenaline. He would catch Eddie Payton at any cost.

For his partner, Art Blake, that meant it could cost them both their lives. Art screamed, "Ahhhh!" as Powers drove between two cars heading the opposite direction.

Jeff pulled even with the fleeing sedan. He yelled out, "Pull over, YOU SONOVABITCH!" And when Eddie answered, "Someone has to stop me!" Powers obliged.

He turned his wheel sharply, slamming into Eddie's sedan, spinning him out and through a corner newsstand, which exploded as Payton's car smashed though it. Then the car went totally out of control, careened off a panel truck and went sideways through all three plate-glass windows of Gomez's Furniture Shop.

Before Eddie could come to his senses, Powers yanked him out through the broken window of his car. Eddie was bruised, bleeding, and half in shock but he recognized the wallet-sized photo that Powers stuck in his face.

Powers couldn't contain his rage anymore. "You did it, didn't you, Eddie? You know where the Chandler kid is, don't you!"

Eddie tried to pull free, but Powers just tightened the grip on his neck even more. Eddie was choking. "You were right, Jeff. You always knew. But I just can't help myself."

Powers knew better. "Bullshit!. Where is he, Eddie?"

Eddie began to whine and Powers started to lose it. He kneed Eddie in the groin, raising him up off his heels, then punched him in the face. "WHERE THE FUCK IS HE?! IS HE STILL ALIVE?" Getting no response, Powers hammered him with blows, working him over deliberately, like a man chopping wood.

Eddie, being the psycho that he was, asked Powers for more. "I deserve punishment," he said.

Frustrated beyond belief, Powers was way over the top, and Eddie's indifference infuriated him. He belted Eddie again and again until Art Blake couldn't stand to watch the beating anymore.

Blake pulled Powers back and was joined by two uniformed cops who were the first to respond to the scene. Powers got in one more kick to Eddie's face before he was pummeled to the ground. The two uniformed cops looked at what was left of Eddie and then at their fellow officer, Jeff Powers. They let him stand up and walk away alone. Powers leaned against their squad car and stared at the police motto emblazoned across the black-and-white door, words he had sworn to obey: *TO PROTECT AND SERVE.*

THE ICE LADY

Here, in the Internal Affairs Division of the Los Angeles Police Department--the I.A., as it was called--Devlin ruled with a hand loaded with a .44 magnum. Men swore she had brass balls bigger than an elephant's. When you stepped into her office, it was never willingly, and few officers ever got out of there without being castrated. This was the coolest and most intelligent black woman you could ever have the misfortune of crossing paths with.

Powers watched her sit and silently rock back and forth in her thick leather chair as she reviewed his folder. He figured the Payton thing had ended his career as a cop and he was just waiting for her confirmation.

Devlin put his folder down on her desk and removed a large red rubber stamp from a side drawer. And then she finally grudgingly told him: "Powers, there's nothing that would have given me a greater pleasure than to have fired your sorry ass off the L.A.P.D." Restrained fury burned in her eyes as she continued, "The fact that you were right about the Chandler boy doesn't excuse anything."

Powers shifted uncomfortably; this was like being in the school principal's office.

She continued, "You know what I hate about this job, Powers?"

He figured he had nothing to lose when he told her, "That they don't let you keep our balls in a jar on your desk?"

She didn't even crack a smile. No one ever got a

59

reaction from black granite. "No, Powers. I hate that this job is political. That when I have a loose cannon like you just begging for jail, someone upstairs can say . . . 'Not sustained.' She slammed the "*CASE CLOSED*" stamp on the cover of his file.

Powers couldn't believe what he'd heard. Just seconds before, he thought his career was history.

Devlin had one more thing to say: "I had your badge in my pocket, Detective Powers. So wherever it is they're sending you, you better toe the line. Because next time, you won't be so lucky. Now get the hell out of my office!" Powers didn't think twice about the invitation to leave, and closed the door behind him as he exited. Standing on the other side of the hall looking directly at him was his old friend, Detective Dan Vaughn.

ONE MORE CHANCE

They greeted each other like two long-lost brothers. Powers was surprised to see him and said so. "Where the hell you been hiding?"

Vaughn would soon let him know. "Not watching you, amigo. Makes me look bad, my old partner stepping in shit with the I.A. Didn't you learn anything from me?"

Powers had learned nearly everything he knew about police work from his ex-partner, but said, "I can take care of myself."

Vaughn knew better. "Bullshit! I had to pull every favor I had to get I.A. off this."

Powers was shocked. "You mean you got me—"

Vaughn interrupted him, "Cut loose? Yeah. The squad I'm with has a lot of juice. Boys upstairs like our work. I've been watching you, son, and I think you're ready for a special assignment."

Powers knew Vaughn never fooled around. "I'm listening."

Vaughn put his arm around his old friend as they walked down the long corridor. "That'd be a fucking first. Here, take this address. We're having a little barbecue. Here's the when and where. Come on out, and meet the guys." Vaughn slapped Powers on the shoulder and started to walk away, but turned around with one last thought. "Trust me, amigo. You're made for this one."

Powers watched him leave, then looked at the business card he'd been handed. On one side was the date and time that Vaughn had written down, but on the other was a sinister cartoon figure of a man with a black cloak drawn across his face holding a dagger in one hand.

STEAKS 'N' BULLETS

The bullet went through the rib-eye steak before it hit the barbecue grill for the second time. The guys all laughed at the makeshift target practice as they all found this to be normal behavior. Just a little workout in the Captain's backyard before lunch, the kind of fun the men in the S.I.S. enjoyed when they got together to blow off steam. The kind of fun that might scare the hell out of anyone else.

They were all there: Cusack, Larson, Angel, Webber, Lloyd, Vaughn, Captain Shafer, and for the first time, Jeff Powers. The S.I.S., their wives, girlfriends, and kids milled around the big yard, laughing, talking, and tilting some beers.

Shafer grabbed another rib-eye and dropped the smoking steak onto Angel's plate. "Thanks, Cap. But I said blood-rare!"

The Cap looked at him steely-eyed. He was a man of strength, a career cop at the top of his game who didn't take kindly to criticism, especially about his cooking. He told Angel, "The way I see it, any steak that isn't burnt to a crisp is blood-fucking rare."

The guys all laughed. Angel took his steak but not without his own comments. "Not for Vaughn, Cap. He likes his meat raw and on the hoof." Powers chimed in with his own good-natured kidding, "Yeah, with tire marks still on it."

But Vaughn, as usual, got the last word on everyone. "Damn straight. You 'ladies' take after me, and you might become real men, someday."

Frank Sacks

The Cap thought that one over for a second. "Are you saying you'd rather have road-kill than one of my gourmet, hand-grilled, top-of-the-line steaks? Think carefully, Vaughn, I'm still your C.O."

Vaughn knew when not to top the boss. He raised his beer in a salute to him. "Here's to the best cook in town!"

Everyone downed their bottles, grabbed a steak, and walked off leaving Mike Lloyd and Dan Vaughn standing together near the bar. Lloyd was the first to grab another drink. He was a big man, with world-weary eyes and drank with the deliberation of someone who needed to get plastered.

Vaughn was reaching across him for another beer when Lloyd asked him, "Dan, how come you never bring your wife to these shindigs anymore?"

Vaughn avoided looking at him when he answered. "You know how it is: Sheila gets a little bored watching you guys wave your dicks in the air."

Lloyd found that real funny, but Vaughn just stared off into the distance and watched Captain Shafer lead Powers into the house for a private conversation of their own.

Powers was surprised at how friendly and relaxed Shafer was around his men. He'd only seen Shafer on duty and knew him to be a man you didn't approach unless he had asked to speak to you first. Powers felt a new sense of pride as Shafer put his arm over his shoulder and shepherded him into his private den.

"You know, Jeff, you cut it pretty close with Eddie Payton. I.A. had you cold."

Powers responded, "Yeah, they told me. Thanks for covering for me."

The look on Shafer's face told Powers the conversation was about to get a lot more serious. He looked straight into Jeff's eyes and said, "We've never done that before. We got you out of that because you're a prime candidate for an elite assignment. But you can also walk away right now, and I can get you reassigned to homicide in another division. Nobody will hold it against you."

Powers still had no idea what it could be. "Cap, I don't even know what the special assignment is yet?" Shafer tried to make him relax a little. "I know, I just don't want you to feel like we've got a gun to your head. Talk to Vaughn, he'll lay out the whole thing for you."

Hearing a sudden flurry of gun shots, Powers looked to the Cap for an explanation. Shafer hardly reacted.

"That's nothing but the boys doin' a little target practice down by the tack shed. You ought to go down and join them. But first help me load up another ice chest."

At the other end of the sprawling backyard was an empty horse shed. All the guys were standing side by side, but they were too drunk for anyone to really call it a line. One at a time, they started taking pistol shots at a half-dozen beer bottles they had stood up on bales of hay forty feet away. It was just more fun and games for this group.

Angel, the transplanted Cuban, took two shots and aced two more bottles. Then he turned to Vaughn, the team leader, and decided now was the time to speak the truth. "Hey, I know he's your boy, *jefe*, but he's not right for the squad. He's a grandstander, y'know? Likes to make the plays himself. I think we need a team player."

Larson felt the same way and said so. "Hell, he wouldn't be on the force if I.A. had their way. I looked at his jacket, he's had almost twenty beefs."

Vaughn was ready. "Most of those charges were 'NOT SUSTAINED.' What's the problem?"

Lloyd was nearly too drunk to talk, but spoke up anyway. "Yeah, but the rest of us managed to get on the squad with only one or two scrapes with I.A." And Angel shot back, "Think of the squad, Dan. We're in the frying pan every time we make a collar. We need to do everything cleaner and better than other cops." Larson agreed: "Powers can't take orders. Period. A guy like that can get one of us killed."

But Vaughn knew better, "I partnered with the guy when he was a cherry gold shield. I was there the first time he took a shot. Look at his street record. He takes care of business."

Larson wouldn't back down, and said, "Sounds like Powers is more ready for this squad than we are."

They laughed, but Vaughn wasn't about to change his mind.

Cusack told him, "Look, this is the best assignment I've ever had. We stop the bad guys, I don't want anything to fuck it up." Angel felt the same way: "Cusack's right, for a change. We're the best of the best. We give repeat offenders a choice: They can go to jail, leave town ... Or die trying," said Larson. Another laugh and a moment passed as they waited for Vaughn's response.

"I know what I'm talking about, people. Back then,

he and I were in a shooting. It went down the way it had to. By the time I.A. shit all over it, I could've kissed my pension goodbye. The kid stood up for me. Covered me. He *belongs* here. And if he wants to try . . . I want him on the team."

Vaughn was dead serious. That was it. The guys knew it and looked at each other, slowly accepting the situation. When they heard Powers walking toward them, they left Vaughn alone and headed back toward the pool area, passing Powers, the new boy, on the way.

Jeff walked up to Vaughn swallowing down the last of his beer. "Cap said you'd fill me in."

Vaughn smiled. He always liked Powers' directness. The kid spoke his mind.

Together, they walked toward the haystacks to set up more bottles. Vaughn spoke first. "Play a little game with me." Powers teased him: "Won't your wife object?" Vaughn laughed, "Yeah, yeah, and fuck *you*, too. Now, listen to me. "Just imagine being able to catch a perp cold, gun in his hand, doing the crime, every single bust you make. Imagine the Force being more interested in putting bad guys away than in covering their ass."

Powers couldn't imagine any such thing and said so. "What have you been drinking?"

Vaughn wasn't kidding. "Imagine a world where you can draw your weapon as soon as you see that the perp is armed, and you don't have to yell, "Police!" until you choose your spot."

Powers didn't get it. "My imagination's not that good."

Vaughn stepped back from the haystack and Powers abruptly decided to test his friend's reflexes. He tossed an empty bottle high in the air, spinning it end over end. Vaughn raised the Desert Eagle as if it was an extension of his arm and fired, exploding the bottle in mid-air. He then turned to Powers with one more thought to consider.

"Your imagination doesn't have to be that good, kid. It's a world I live in. It's all real, I live it every day . . . "

PRACTICE MAKES PERFECT

BLAM! BLAM! BLAM! were the sounds of the bullets ripping through the face of a cardboard target. The S.I.S. was in motion, practicing as a team on the L.A.P.D. Combat Pistolcraft Range. It was a maze of phony buildings and barricades, with pop-up targets representing good guys and bad.

Vaughn and Powers moved through it as a pair, firing and pausing with practiced ease. Between reloads of fresh clips, they exchanged knowing looks and a little conversation, though it required yelling to overcome the pistol noise around them and especially the sounds of the .50 caliber Desert Eagle cannon Vaughn called his own.

"You've already met most of the team, now you can see them work."

Powers looked farther down the range as gunfire roared throughout the area. He saw Angel, Larson, and Cusack move professionally through the course.

"They're good. Wouldn't want them against *me*," he said. Vaughn knew they were better than good and said so. "That's the point. We take the bad boys off the street. It's no fucking rogue outfit, either. We're not talking clan or some neo-Nazi bullshit. We're an official, elite unit, operating under official Department policy."

They moved on to the next set of targets. Powers kicked open a door and fired first, taking the head off a

dummy target marked "hostage." Vaughn stepped in
through the doorway and nailed the real target—"the
criminal"—between the eyes. The force of his high-
calibered gun blew a three-inch-wide hole in the head
of the cardboard dummy. It made Powers wonder
what it would do to the real thing?

THE S.I.S. BRIEFING ROOM

Powers followed Vaughn as he quickly entered Parker Center, the downtown L.A.P.D. headquarters. He had to quicken his pace to keep up with Dan, who was unlike most officers entering this building. The other men in blue stopped to talk with friends but Vaughn kept moving.

They walked past the elevators, opened an unmarked door, and descended two flights of stairs to a sub-basement level. Walking down a long corridor with dozens of padlocked storage rooms on each side, they went through another unmarked door and down one more flight of stairs.

At the bottom of the stairwell was yet another unmarked door. Vaughn took out his key and let Powers step in first.

To his surprise, Powers found himself standing in a high-tech room. Vaughn motioned for him to take one of the empty seats.

Although they were deep inside Police Headquarters, in the middle of downtown Los Angeles, it was a bunker very few cops had ever heard of and even fewer had entered. Powers looked around, taking it all in at once. The concrete room was a thousand square feet in size. At one end, a large six-foot rear-screen projection apparatus came to life. Vaughn flicked a podium switch and the lights dimmed. At the other end of the room, a twenty-foot-long control panel lit up. It was divided into three sections, each panel containing fifty different switches and lights and a sunken

TV screen connected to computers that tied them into the main L.A.P.D. computer located five floors above.

The room was lit by rows of fluorescent lights. On each side of the projection screen in the front were chalk boards and, next to them, two cork boards stapled with black-and-white pictures of crime victims and their suspected perps.

The room had five rows of movable desks and twenty chairs. The equipment was very much state-of-the-art police communications gear and unlike anything Jeff Powers had seen except when he'd made a visit to FBI headquarters in Washington. Not even L.A.'s infamous SWAT team had anything like this. The room was soundproof, air-conditioned, and had a battery of fax machines, telephones, a copier, and a bank of interconnecting hardware capable of screening slides, film, and vhs tapes.

This was the secret briefing room for the Special Investigation Section. A room that only a handful of the 900 L.A.P.D. employees above them even knew existed as anything other than a rumor. It reminded Jeff of a war room . . . and it was.

Vaughn didn't waste any time. "We're hunter-trackers. An eighteen-man unit, with three six-man squads working round-the-clock surveillance. We target high-profile criminals, and track 'em until they commit another felony—"Powers had to interrupt, "Just felonies?"

Vaughn continued, "No loose change, Jeff. We want to put these guys away for a long time." He handed Jeff two photos. "These are the sweethearts we're targeting now. Billy Nash, Johnny Speer, and the 4th Street Goons. They rob banks, and they hurt people.

That's their job. Our job is to stop them."

Powers had to interrupt again. This was wild. "What? With pictures?"

Vaughn let the kid tease him as he hit another switch on the podium.An undercover video surveillance tape of the perps appeared on the big screen next to them.

Vaughn continued, "You're thinking like a beat cop, kid. This is real surveillance. Crooks like this develop. We follow them, learn how they work, and then shut 'em down." Powers was impressed. This was hot. "Pretty intense. How many cases do you work at a time?"

"One. Until we put them away."

The answer blew Jeff's mind.

Powers had seen and heard a lot in his eight years on the force, but nothing could top what Dan Vaughn had just told him. This was more than just serious. This was like a cop's fantasy come true. "How come I never heard of the S.I.S.?"

Vaughn told him, "We're low profile. Officially, even the Mayor doesn't know we exist."

Powers looked puzzled. He said, "You want *me* on this squad? I mean, everybody has me down as bad news. I'm not exactly what you'd call 'elite,'"

Vaughn smiled. He knew he had Jeff's attention now. "You're working with the wrong people, Jeff. What used to get you in trouble, will get you a round of beers with S.I.S."

Powers laughed to himself at the irony of what Vaughn had just said, until Captain Shafer entered the room.

Shafer closed and locked the door behind him. He

looked over to Jeff. "Vaughn making everything sound attractive, Powers?"

Powers nodded and spoke up. "Yeah, where do I sign?" Shafer sat down on the desk in front of him. His mood changed as he thought about what he was going to say. "Let's back up a minute, Jeff. There are no showboats on this squad: we can't afford the risk. I know your record, Jeff, and so do the guys on the squad. If I let you in, you'd better fly right. We operate under strict guidelines. Mistakes mean coming home in a bag."

Powers got the point. "Loud and clear, Cap. If I fuck up here, it's not just my ass, I have a team depending on me."

It was a tense moment. The final decision would be Shafer's and he was thinking about it. Powers could feel Shafer's eyes as if they were drilling straight through to the back of his skull. He was relieved when the Cap finally cracked a smile and said, "You're right, Dan. I like him." He turned to Powers, "We've got two rules in the S.I.S., Detective Powers. We target the most dangerous criminals and take those animals off the streets for good."

Powers asked, "And the second?"

Vaughn answered, "We keep quiet."

Shafer stood up and extended his hand. "Welcome to the S.I.S."

KELLY

Kelly Daniels was known by many names, depending on your point of view: as a reporter for the *Los Angeles Chronicle*, she was known by her colleagues to be aggressive, abrasive, underpaid, frustrated, and after two years still working the West Side section that covered everything from church announcements to small crime, but never the big news. . . .

To her boss, Max, she was an up-and-comer who would be writing feature stories in another three years—important news, at that . . . that is, if she was still around and had not had her butt fired for mouthing off to the wrong person. . . .

To Jeff Powers, Kelly Daniels was an enigma. At five-seven, a hundred and twelve pounds, with green eyes and beautiful dark, long red hair, she was pure fire and a hard-on from the second he'd met her. It had been in a bar they both frequented near the Marina.

Upon meeting, Kelly had pegged him all wrong that first night. She had thought they might have a fling—but that was all. His long hair and offbeat style had totally fooled her.

From the moment they locked eyes, neither wanted to talk shop: There were far more interesting things below the surface they were anxious to feel out. To their mutual surprise, they not only screwed each other's brains out but discovered that each was a serious professional dedicated to their career. From that first night on, they decided to keep their professional lives out of the bedroom and, for that matter, out of the house they had ultimately come to share for the last two years.

As Jeff had spent the last twelve hours in a basement under Parker Center, he was surprised Kelly was still up when he walked in past midnight. He took his shirt and pants off in the bedroom and stepped up behind her wearing only his jockey shorts. Rubbing against her back made it tough for her to concentrate on a story with a morning deadline. But when she didn't look up from her computer, he pushed against her a little harder and started massaging her shoulders. *This isn't fair,,* she thought.

Not wanting to completely lose her concentration, she did manage to say, "Hello, sweetheart."

Jeff leaned down over her shoulder and kissed her neck. He eased one hand down the front of her bra. She pulled forward. Now was not the time.

He asked, "You gonna work all night?" He kissed her cheek, breaking her concentration.

Her smile was a mix of desire and exasperation. "The answer is yes. Let me finish these three sentences. . . . This piece has to hit the late edition."

Jeff lowered his hand one more time onto her breast and squeezed her nipple. She reluctantly pulled forward again. She loved how he touched her.

He teased her. "I like having you here, even when you're working," he murmured. "Nice to have someone to come home to, y'know?"

Kelly struggled to hit another few keys. "Don't start . . ." But she knew he wasn't going to stop.

He smiled. "I didn't say a thing. Not even Vegas."

It was all she could take. She turned away from the

computer, grabbed him gently by the hair, and firmly planted a deep kiss on his mouth to hopefully cool him off for the moment. Then she said, "No. We are not getting married."

Kelly started typing again but continued to talk. "You were the one who said we shouldn't have to choose between our jobs and each other. You were right."

He began to massage her shoulders again. "I'm always right. I hate it."

Kelly knew she had to finish the assignment now or never. "It's tough enough as it is, Jeff. You know how hard it is for a reporter to listen to all the stuff you bring home and *not* use it in a story?"

His hands continued to rub her shoulders and now her neck. "Hey, we made a deal, Kel: Nothing leaves the room, right? We can blow off steam, and not worry about it."

She listened to his words carefully and then couldn't hold back any longer. What she had to say now was going to definitely change the mood, but she couldn't help it. "Then explain Eddie Payton."

Powers couldn't handle it and tried to escape. "Eddie who?"

Kelly pushed them both away from the table and stood up. "Very smooth, Jeff. Eddie Payton, you know, the sick bastard you lost your badge over? Max told me Eddie left me a message, so I could get some photos. Nobody knew when they were going to release the sonofabitch. But you were right there. And my answering machine was rewound."

Powers was in deep shit. He could forget about sex.

This was real trouble. He tried to take a defensive posture. "He chops up little kids, Kelly. I mean, hell. . ."

Kelly already knew that, "He's a psychotic shit, Jeff, but that doesn't change what you did to him."

This was definitely an uncomfortable moment for both of them. Powers knew she was right. He decided to take the man's way out. "I'm sorry. I crossed the line. It won't happen again."

They were words she had hoped to hear. Kelly stepped closer to him, teasing, "That's not good enough," and kissed him again. This time it was a slow, blistering kiss.

Powers recognized a good apology when it worked, and kissed her throat and her shoulders, working his way down her body. She loved it. He lifted her in his arms and stepped toward the bedroom.

"And I didn't lose my badge, bright eyes. I just got reassigned."

Kelly couldn't believe it. "Where?"

Powers rolled his eyes. He'd blown it again, but he couldn't let his big mouth stop the momentum, and asked her, "You *really* want to talk shop now?" They kissed again and he kept walking toward the bedroom, saying, "Now, where was I?" She knew exactly where and said so, "You were about to apologize the hell out of me. . . ."

HOME ALONE

Vaughn walked into his house and turned off the silent alarm. He smiled to himself over some inner thought and called out to his wife, "Hey, Sheila . . . I'm home," but there was no response and yet it didn't seem to surprise him. He threw his sport coat over the couch in the living room and picked up a half-bottle of Cutty and a glass on the way into the den.

His house was early-seventies Rancho Santa Fe—not bad for a cop, but they'd been lucky and bought before the market started climbing. The place was sort of folksy, with a wooden mantle in the living room and beams across the ceiling. The den in particular had a nice feel to it, more like a place you'd find in a country retreat.

Vaughn sank into the sofa, removed his Desert Eagle and shoulder holster, and popped the clip to be sure it was empty. He took his ankle holster off and left the .38 intact within it. As he poured himself two inches of whiskey he gazed at the two framed pictures sitting on the coffee table in front of him.

In one, Sheila appeared in a head shot with shoulder-length hair. She was an attractive brunette but the picture was just a simple head shot more reminiscent of a college 8 X 10 glossy. Next to it was an entirely different Sheila, this one taken in their backyard by Dan himself. He'd told her to put on her smallest two-piece, and after they'd both had a few drinks, he'd started taking pictures. This was his favorite shot, although it was quite unlike her. He'd had to get her drunk before she loosened up enough and started posing like a cheap pin-up girl. It was sexy, all right, with her ass turned up toward the camera. The look on her face was more an invitation than a party picture. It was a look meant for his eyes only and not the kind of picture most men would keep out in the open—if it was their wife.

Dan picked it up in his hand and leaned back in the sofa. His first sip on the Cutty emptied half the glass, and he didn't hesitate to pour himself another, even taller one.

He put the picture down and picked up the .38 again. Methodically, and without thinking, he emptied the rounds from the cylinder and slapped it back in place. He cocked the hammer back. Holding it carefully with both hands, he aimed it directly at her. "You miss me, baby? Think about me? I think about you. Every time I call Liquor Locker for a fucking delivery." The whiskey was hitting home and Dan Vaughn was feeling rather bitter. "Hell, I think about you all the time."

It was obvious that Sheila wouldn't be coming home tonight—or any other night. Vaughn kept on talking to the picture as if to create life, where none existed. "You think Powers'll make it? I stuck my neck out for the kid. You never stuck your neck out for me— What? All right, you couldn't live with it. With *what*? My life! Never loved me enough to try."

Dan Vaughn was deep in his own world and completely alone. His finger slowly tightened on the trigger, his emotions inside squeezing him even harder. "Jesus, baby, I think about you all the time. I miss you, baby. I miss you real bad . . ."

And with that, he slowly squeezed the trigger until he heard the click, click, and then one more empty shot to her head. He was feeling all the pain of a marriage that would never be put back together.

The pistol suddenly seemed impossibly heavy to hold, and he let it down slowly, his head sinking with it. He was alone in the house. The sun was nearly down and long shadows were cast across the room, across a man sitting among the ruins of his life.

BILLY NASH AND THE 4TH STREET GANG

It was plain and simple. Billy Nash was a jive-talking black asshole. He would have robbed his mother and raped his sister . . . if he'd known who they were. He grew up on the streets of St. Louis. It was an infinitely better place than his home, where his dad took great pleasure in beating the hell out of him.

Some guys liked to snatch purses, and some preferred pimping, and some got their rocks off holding up cheap little liquor stores, like Tyrone Deacon. But Billy was slick. Super slick. He loved the game. Any game. You wanna play cards? You want to bet the horses, the dogs, the trotters? Christ, Billy Nash would take a bet he could piss in a urinal for five minutes straight. He'd drink a gallon of water and wait till his bladder had near burst before he'd try the game on you.

But games like that only made a fiver here, or maybe ten, if he was lucky. Times got to be that ten bucks wouldn't buy a real dime's worth of crack. The recession had hit everything, except drugs. So, Billy wanted to turn to the bigger con, like some dudes he knew who ran stolen cars across state lines. Now, those were real hustlers to Billy. They'd grab a new Camero out of St. Louis and hustle it out of town, have it across the state line and broken down into new parts that would be sold to junk yards, gas stations, even new-car dealerships.

Billy got cynical real fast, watching so-called honest

people take the hot stuff when the price was right. But Billy got caught by the Feds, and Billy did time. Lot's of time. One thing about jail though, it was a real learning experience. If there was something you wanted to know about robbery, forgery, or murder, at least you were surrounded by professionals.

But what always made the biggest impression on the cons in jail were the goddam bank robbers. If you wanted a big rep in prison, then you had to go rob a couple of banks. These were the guys everybody looked up to, and Billy was no different. He caught the bug real bad. So, he learned everything he could while he did his time. And he swore that when he got out, he was going to California to rob banks. He was gonna be big-time. No more little shakedowns for Billy Nash.

And although Billy was slick and pure jive, when he set his mind to it he moved straight ahead. Like a train goin' down a track. Within three days after walking out of the Greyhound bus station in downtown L.A., he had himself a gun, a place to stay, and a brand-new stolen car with phony plates.

In prison Billy had also found out that there was a learning curve to everything, including robbing banks. So he knew it would be a lot safer to start small. The first joint he knocked over wasn't even a bank, it was an S&L. One of those small ones that catered to elderly people in the neighborhood, who kept their jumbo CDs in it, didn't need a checking account, and liked to stop by once a week just to talk to the people who worked there.

Billy was in and out of the place in less than two minutes. He had twenty-five hundred in cash to prove it. The video cameras got a good look at Billy that day, but in L.A., the bank-robbing capital of the world, Billy was just a new face, he hardly made an impression, being just one of ten bank robberies that day.

Billy really liked the new game, and he went back for more. In the next three weeks, he robbed three other S&Ls. The L.A.P.D. saw it as a pattern, and decided it was time to check the guy out.

For Billy, it was time to move up and hit a real bank. But first he needed to kick back for a week or so and make some new friends. So he found himself a nice young white hooker to call his own. Then he went looking for some real guns and to see if he could put his own gang together.

He met Johnny Speer in a whorehouse down in Compton. They were both jive and knew the game. Speer liked to hang out with another white girl named Mary Baines; she had stringy hair, thin legs, but did she have a set.

What a team! They were like the Manson version of the Brady bunch. But what Billy Nash needed now was a pro, a guy he knew wouldn't hesitate to blow some fuckin' bank guard away, just in case.

Nash found the perfect man: Vincent Simmons. He was like the old man of the group. Christ, he must have been pushing fifty-five or so. But it didn't matter. His rep stood him tall. The guy had done nearly twenty years in one slammer or another. Nash was impressed; this guy not only had robbed banks, he'd actually blown up safes before they got to be so big you'd blow the building before you could get one of the new ones to open up. And Vince was looking to do two, maybe three real jobs. If they were lucky, that would mean twenty or thirty thousand for each of them every time they made a score, tax free.

Vincent Simmons and Billy Nash knew exactly which bank they would hit first: American Fidelity Trust on the corner of 14th and Broadway, only blocks from the heart of downtown Los Angeles. What they didn't know was that an informer who sold them a shotgun and an uzzi had told the cops about these two. And, once Nash and Simmons were spotted together, the information had been passed on to Captain Shafer's special group, the S.I.S.

For eight days and nights, Vaughn's unit had tailed first Nash, and then Simmons. Initially, nothing seemed to come together. The two perps weren't spending much time with each other, and it looked as if Nash was more interested in his other friends and staying up half the night partying.

But on a Friday morning in the first week of July, Cusack and Larson had watched Nash leave his apartment with what looked like a shotgun rolled in newspaper. Newspaper that he very carefully placed in the trunk of his car. So Larson called it in, and within forty minutes the rest of the squad were tailing Nash through the gritty, colorful streets of Hollywood.

Nash picked up the rest of his new gang; Mary Baines, Vince, his young girlfriend, Daisy, and Johnny Speer.

Angel had watched them for the last twenty minutes and decided it was time to pull back and call it in: "Center to Quarterback; the ball's heading your way." Two blocks ahead of him, Vaughn held up a pair of

Frank Sacks

powerful binoculars and watched Nash's car approaching. He had the feeling it was no joy ride and passed them off to Powers to have a look.

Vaughn picked up the mic. "Copy, Center, Quarterback has the ball." Vaughn turned back to Lloyd, who was sitting in the rear seat looking at a picture of Nash. Vaughn laughed. "Billy Nash, ugly as life. Let me take a look." Lloyd handed over the picture of Nash.

Jeff watched as Nash drove past them. Vaughn handed him the picture and pulled away from the curb. As Vaughn followed, he was very precise in judging his distance and stayed no less than a hundred and fifty feet away. Powers studied the picture for a moment. "Yeah, that's Nash. Plus a new one I've never seen before."

Vaughn continued moving through the traffic with a perfect sense of timing. He kept the distance between them just right. The unmarked S.I.S. car was always hidden by other cars but never so far back that it could lose them.

Vaughn was getting the feeling again. "Here we go."

Powers was nervous, though he wasn't sure why. He'd done surveillance before, but there was something about this crew that made it all very different. There was more of a purpose to it all, a sense of waiting for the inevitable. He asked Vaughn, "You check the computer on these guys, boss?"

Vaughn didn't take his eyes off Nash's car but answered Powers' question: "Not our job, Jeff. Cap puts together the intelligence. We track 'em and sack 'em."

Lloyd was curious, though. "Punch 'em up,

Powers," he said.

Jeff tapped the computer keyboard on the dash despite Vaughn's disapproving look. He read it aloud: "Nash has an outstanding felony rap from Texas. Assault and battery. We could bag him right now and get on to the next bad guy."

Vaughn was vaguely amused at the idea and said so. "Fuck Texas. You want to hand Nash over to some Fort Worth Wyatt Earp? Nash'll be out and back in L.A. in six months."

Powers didn't know what to say. He just thought, to himself, that this way of doing business was going to be very different than anything he'd ever experienced before.

Vaughn looked in the rearview and checked on Lloyd. "You okay back there, pal? You look like you partied a little hard last night."

Lloyd was definitely hung over, but that was nothing new for him and he said so. "I can handle it."

Powers was the first to notice Nash slowing down as he drove past American Fidelity Trust. "Look at that," he said.

Vaughn drove past them and quickly turned at the corner. He pulled over and parked, looking back at Nash's car, now idling right in front of the bank's main entrance. "Yeah. Just an ordinary bunch of citizens trying to choose a new bank to rob."

Nash suddenly pulled out into traffic and turned the same corner, passing their car, but Vaughn didn't follow. Powers looked confused. Vaughn could see the question on his friend's face, and answered it with confidence, "He'll be back, but with a new car."

Vaughn was definitely in his element, and Powers thought his instincts even sharper than they'd been years before. Vaughn picked up the mic again, "Fullback, this is your Quarterback. Pick up the ball."

Passing by them on their right, Powers could see Larson talking to them, "Roger that, Quarterback. Fullback has the ball."

Nash and the trailing S.I.S. car turned the next corner and were out of sight. "How do you know this is it, Dan? I mean, right now?" asked Powers.

"I got a feeling, kid. But they've got an M.O., they steal a car, use it at the bank, and swap back to their own."

Lloyd leaned forward. "So if they steal a car in the next couple of minutes, we know it's showtime."

Vaughn pulled out his Desert Eagle to check the clip and said, "The last few minutes are always the longest."

Less than a mile away, Larson watched Billy Nash park behind a beat-up Ford Fairlane. Nash had the door jimmied open and the car hot-wired in less than thirty seconds. In moments, the gang had switched cars and were heading back toward the bank.

Cusack picked up the mic. "Center to Team. The ball is in play. Repeat, the ball is in play. White Ford sedan. We will carry the ball to the end zone. We have five players on the visiting team."

Vaughn listened impassively to Cusack's words and then responded, "Roger. Quarterback moving in now. Close off the back doors." He dropped the mic and slid the action back on his gun, chambering a round. He turned to Jeff with a slightly wry smile on his face and asked, "You ready to go in?"

Powers was not ready. "Now? Nash isn't even here yet."

Vaughn liked surprises, and said, "Imagine the look on Nash's face when he finds he's got S.I.S. instead of hostages."

Powers' mind was racing. "I don't know, man, sounds like entrapment."

Vaughn didn't care. "We're not *asking* him to rob the fucking bank, we just know he will. Let's go save some lives."

There was no turning back. Jeff knew he'd better catch up quickly. "Okay, okay," he said, and got out of the car.

Vaughn was totally in charge. There was no question about who was giving the orders. He turned to Lloyd, commanding, "Mike, give Angel some backup. Don't let their car get away." Lloyd's eyes were as clouded as his mind, and Vaughn snapped at him, "Hey, buddy. Get your head out of your ass!"

Lloyd was worried, "Dan, the bank's too fucking crowded. It's Friday. People could get killed."

Vaughn got hot. "I don't have time for this shit, man. You want out, or you want to do your fucking job?"

Lloyd knew he shouldn't have opened his mouth. "No, Dan, it's cool. I'm in."

He watched Vaughn and Powers move across the street and into the bank. Lloyd was worried, really worried; but it was too late for all of them. He got behind the wheel and had to wait only a few seconds before he saw the gang's white Ford pull up, shadowed by Angel's car.

Across the street, Larson pulled his car over to block any chance of leaving an escape route open. Cusack was riding shotgun and appropriately squeezed a few more shells into his Remington Pump-Action. From their vantage point, they could see Nash and Mary getting out of the car. Mary was suddenly looking very pregnant.

Larson knew better. "Betcha lunch Nash takes Mary in, baby and all."

Cusack wasn't fooled. "You still owe me lunch from the Bears game."

Larson challenged him, "Double or nothing." Cusack had sucked him in.

"Deal! But you're not getting away with McDonald's, pal."

The two laughed. It was more like they were sitting around a living room telling jokes . . . and not waiting for a bank robbery to go down.

Two hundred feet away, Angel wasn't exactly in the same mood. He nervously squeezed a grip exerciser, waiting for the show to start. He picked up the mic. "If these guys weren't so fuckin' scary, they'd be funny. Locos, eh? Hitting a bank on a Friday afternoon."

Cusack responded over the radio, "Sounds like something your home boys would do, *bandejo*."

Angel laughed and said, "It's against regulations to make racial remarks to fellow officers, you in-bred, white-trash motherfucker!"

More laughter over the radio. These two had been at each other's throats for years.

Cusack checked his gun and picked up the mic. "I hope you're ready, greaseball."

Angel checked his own gun, but kept an eye on the bank. He could see Nash. "Born ready, *gringo*." Angel put the mic down and eased his door open to move out.

Nash, Mary, and Vincent had gotten out of their car. Mary's loose-fitting top barely accommodated her pregnant belly. Nash leaned over and gave Johnny a deadly, rattlesnake glare. "Keep it runnin'. We'll be in an' out real quick." He threatened him, "You chicken-shit on me, and I'll hunt you down, boy."

Nash's intimidating glare made Johnny Speer grab the wheel a little tighter. He gave Nash a fearful nod. Mary was getting impatient, "C'mon, let's go. I'm gonna break my fuckin' water out here!"

Nash really dug this bitch, she was a player. He put his arm over her shoulder and then led the way with Vince walking behind them.

Mary's "baby" suddenly moved and she quickly adjusted her pregnant stomach. Nash told her, "Don't lose the baby, sugar. She's real important to me."

Mary knew what she was doing. "Me, too, Billy. Don't worry." She smiled and kissed him, and then they walked into the bank together.

Larson shook his head, he didn't like the count. "Shit. There's three of them. Nash never takes three. Vaughn's a man short."

Cusack wasn't concerned in the least. "Our gig's the getaway car. Vaughn won't mind three against two. He'd just say it sharpens his edge."

Larson wasn't so sure.

Inside the getaway car, Johnny kept the motor running, waiting nervously. He glanced in the rearview mirror and watched Daisy, a thin-looking fifteeen-year-old with too much eye shadow on. She picked up Nash's shotgun off the back seat next to her.

Johnny told her, "Don't touch that, Daisy. Nash'll get pissed!" Like a child, the look on her face was more of a pout. She shoved the gun aside. Johnny thought he'd really like a taste of her: "Wanna party later?" She considered the idea; she thought he was cute even with his lascivious, cracked-tooth smile. She gave him a sexy look way beyond her years.

Inside the bank, Vaughn had positioned himself about seventy feet from the front door. There were at least twenty customers and a dozen large desks spread out over the enormous main floor. Toward the front double-door entrance, a single armed guard stood watching the day's business in front of him. Powers stood at the last of three tables that were placed in a line down the middle of the bank's marble floor. He took a withdrawal slip from the counter and pretended to fill it out.

Nash, Mary, and Vincent entered the bank trying to act nonchalant. Mary walked up to the first table and began filling out a slip, while her friends watched. After spotting the guard, the three of them split up without attracting any attention, but Nash kept his eye on the guard's position.

Vaughn moved behind a metal sign stand and when he was sure Nash was looking the other way, he eased his gun out of his waistband and held it behind his back.

Nash moved over to one end of the long teller's

counter and with his back to the wall he was ready. He took one last look around and then gave a "go" nod. With one quick move, Nash jerked out an uzzi machine gun and yelled out his commands, "All right, EVERY-BODY DOWN! THIS IS A STICKUP!" The bank guard immediately reacted and drew his revolver.

It was the wrong decision. Billy turned on him and squeezed the trigger. Half a dozen rounds blanketed the guard's chest, sending blood spilling out through the holes in his uniform as he was riddled with bullets.

Vince's head turned one way, then another, his eyes darting about. There were so damn many people screaming, yelling, and scrambling for cover that he didn't know which way to look first.

Mary calmly reached under her blouse for her "baby," and pulled out a sawed-off semi-automatic shotgun wrapped in a pillow. She turned to the startled woman nearby and told her, "Move your ass or this baby'll blow your fucking head off!"

Powers and Vaughn had their guns out, ready to fire, but were blocked by the customers scrambling between them and the robbers. Vince saw them and fired his 9-mm Sig-Sauer. His first shot hit a man near Vaughn, causing him to fall onto Vaughn's gun hand and preventing the Detective from getting a shot off. Vaughn pushed the man aside and moved forward.

Mary saw Powers draw his gun and unloaded two shotgun shells that exploded huge chunks of wood off the desk next to him. He dove for cover as she fired again. Nash also trained his machine gun on Powers and squeezed the trigger. A dozen bullets hit all around him, but Jeff was protected by the heavy mahogany of the desk.

In seconds, Nash loaded a fresh clip into his uzzi, and Vaughn moved again, working his way closer.

At the same time, in another part of the city, a "211 in progress" flashed across a police dispatcher's computer screen. The rookie manning the desk leaned forward into the mic at her station. "All units in the vicinity, we have a 211 in progress at American Fidelity Trust, corner of 14th and Broadway."

Her supervisor quickly stepped up behind. He was a silver-haired Captain. He covered the mic with his hand and told her, "Cancel that 211; code it Wildfire, they'll handle it." She understood the command but not the term "wildfire." She hadn't been at the job long enough to know about the S.I.S. She wondered how anyone could ignore an incoming emergency like this.

Looking up at the Captain's face, she realized it wasn't the time to ask questions. Calmly, he told her again, "That's an order, officer. Code it Wildfire; the boys in the field will understand."

She did as she was told. "All units, this is dispatch, cancel response to the 211, code name Wildfire, repeat, code name Wildfire."

On the street in front of the bank, Johnny's nerves were fried by all the gunfire he heard inside. This was all he could take. He'd deal with Nash later if the guy was still alive. "We're getting outta here, Daisy." One look at her face and he knew she wasn't about to disagree.

As Johnny pulled out, Larson and Angel did the

same. All three cars collided at the corner only fifty feet from the bank's entrance. Johnny tried to back up, but Larson's car smashed into his back side. When he tried to throw it into forward, Angel drove up and had him pinned. In seconds, Larson, Cusack, Angel, and Lloyd were behind their cars and had their guns aimed directly at Johnny Speer.

His next move was fatal. He reached for a gun in the glove compartment.

The four S.I.S. squad members opened up in unison. Thirty rounds drove into the car at the same instant. Cusack's shotgun blasts took out the side windows first, showering Daisy with glass as she cowered down in the seat. Bullets flew all around her, tearing into the seats. In the front, Johnny was hit in the throat. As he clutched it with both hands, five more rounds went through the door and hit him in the legs and arm.

The front windshield shattered as a dozen more rounds blew through it and him in the next instant. Two more shots from the rear slammed into Johnny's skull from behind and pushed his dead body into the steering wheel. Daisy couldn't stand it. She freaked out and put her hands around Nash's shotgun lying next to her. Just as the gunfire ceased, she raised it above the seat.

As Lloyd moved in closer, he saw the barrel of the shotgun rise into view above the door. He emptied five more rounds into the back seat. The high-powered slugs penetrated the thin metal and hit Daisy, knocking her backwards. Two more shots from the other direction caught her in the chest and ended it all.

The gunfire inside the bank erupted again, and

although everyone outside had finally stopped firing, they stayed behind their cars waiting for one of the gang to come running out the front door.

Inside, Nash dropped down to one knee to put the last clip in his uzzi. Mary tried to finish off Vaughn but was a second too late; he fired three rounds into her chest. The impact blew her totally off her feet and backwards into the teller's marble counter, where she dropped to the floor.

At that moment, Nash screamed out, "MARY!" and with vengeance in his eyes fired almost the whole clip at Vaughn, who dove behind another desk, rolled out of the line of fire, and was up on one knee in the same move. He fired six .50 caliber shots into Nash.

The huge shells blew Nash's chest apart. He was dead before he fell to the ground and let one hand go of the uzzi, spraying his last shots wildly. One of them hit a young blond teller in the shoulder and knocked her down. Dark red blood poured from her shoulder wound, saturating her white blouse.

Vaughn dropped the empty clip from his Desert Eagle and had it reloaded in seconds as Powers and Vincent continued firing at each other. Vaughn stopped moving in, and with a rock-steady aim squeezed the trigger of his gun without releasing it until he'd emptied five rounds into the older perp. The intensity of all those hits propelled Vincent a dozen feet. As he tumbled backwards, his arms waved up and down from the impact. His body finally crashed through the plate-glass door behind and he wound up dead on the floor, half in and half out of the bank door.

Outside, Lloyd was the first to move in closer. He knew both occupants in the getaway car had to be dead. He opened the back door slowly and saw little Daisy staring up at him, both eyes still open. It was a look he would remember until the day he died. She had not been hit in the face and Lloyd couldn't believe how young she was. He took the shotgun out of her lifeless hands and pumped it to unload the chamber, but the gun was empty.

Lloyd's mind began to spin. He'd killed this young girl for no reason. If only he'd waited a moment longer before firing . . . If he had just had a second to yell out to drop the weapon . . . If, if only she wasn't so young. He slammed her shotgun down on the trunk so hard the wooden stock broke into pieces. His face took on a look of near-insanity.

Cusack called his name to get him back. "Lloyd . . . Hey, Lloyd."

But he was gone, and never would come back. Lloyd drew his revolver, aiming it at Cusack. "Don't move!" he ordered. "We killed her, *I* killed her. Her gun, her goddam gun was empty. EMPTY!"

Larson slowly started to raise his own pistol. Lloyd turned on him, ready to fire. He'd lost it. He yelled again, "Don't move!"

Larson wasn't sure what to do, he'd never had a cop draw a gun on him. No one moved.

Inside, the shooting had stopped, but it looked as if a bomb had gone off. A dozen people were injured, three would-be bank robbers were dead and so was the bank guard, and one customer. Two other employees had serious gunshot wounds.

The rest of the employees and customers slowly began to get to their feet. Several women started to sob, while most of the others were so shocked they couldn't utter a sound.

Powers and Vaughn held their guns trained on Billy and Mary as they approached them. Both were lying in giant pools of blood on the marble floor. Vaughn leaned down to touch each of them and put two fingers on the side of their necks to try to detect a pulse. There was none. He looked over to Jeff, and simply shook his head to indicate they were dead. It was something Jeff had already known. Even in the old days, he'd never seen anyone left alive after Vaughn finished shooting.

Jeff holstered his gun and in a daze moved toward the front door. As he passed Vaughn he said, "I'll call an ambulance."

When Powers stepped outside, Lloyd swung his gun toward him. Jeff stopped, unable to understand what was happening. But Vaughn was already at his friend's side.

Lloyd's face said it all. He called out to Vaughn, pleadingly, as if to ask for mercy, "Dan. Why couldn't we just arrest them? Why?"

Vaughn slowly moved away from Powers. Vaughn said nothing. The look on his face was one of both pity and contempt for his team member.

Lloyd lowered his gun slightly, then cocked the hammer. "I can't do it, Dan. I'm no good anymore. Not to you ... not to the squad ... not to myself. I want out."

Powers slowly moved to position himself behind

Lloyd, who continued to try to connect with his leader: "Dan . . . I can't, I can't do this anymore . . ."

Powers wasn't sure whether Lloyd could see him, but leaped at him anyway, knocking the gun aside and tackling him. Cusack and Larson wrestled Lloyd against the side of Angel's car. Vaughn rushed over and commanded, "Get him in the car, get him the hell outta here. NOW!" Lloyd looked at him one last time. Vaughn told him what he needed to hear: "Okay, pal. You win. You're out." Vaughn slapped the roof of the car, and Angel took off with Powers and Cusack in the back seat with Lloyd. Without hesitation, Dan turned to Larson and told him, "Call it in."

Less than a mile away, Captain Shafer waited in his squad car. Four more regular units were parked in a line behind him. Shafer picked up the mic. "Roger, we copy." He turned to his Sergeant behind the wheel and said, "Roll it." The five black-and-whites and an ambulance wheeled out in unison. They roared down the street with their red light bars revolving and sirens blaring.

When Kelly Daniels arrived fifteen minutes later, the crime scene was still chaotic with paramedics and ambulances taking care of the wounded and the dead. A huge crowd had formed, but she walked through them and into the cordoned-off area. Two of the paramedics were wheeling out the blond bank teller with the shoulder wound.

Kelly pulled out her Press Pass and asked one of them about the wounded girl. "Hi, Kelly Daniels, *L.A. Chronicle*. Can I talk to her?"

The paramedic was obviously stressed as he helped

his partner lift the gurney into the ambulance. "She's in bad shape. It's like a war zone in there. Lucky more cops didn't get hit."

Kelly's ears perked up. "You mean they were *inside* the bank??"

The paramedic didn't have time for any interviews. "Yeah, and this lady's gonna be inside the morgue if we don't move."

Brushing her aside, he and another paramedic slammed the doors shut and quickly drove off.

Kelly surveyed the scene as several other sealed body bags were placed in a vehicle from the Coroner's Office. She looked toward the bank entrance and decided to make her move. As she walked toward the front entrance, two officers blocked her way. Flashing her I.D. got her nowhere.

"I've got a right to go in there!" she insisted. They didn't budge. She spotted a familiar face and tried to get his attention. "Captain Kramer!" Kramer looked up and smiled, but he remained behind the barrier working with members of the crime lab, taking pictures and samples.

Kelly worked her way closer, and after a few minutes the Captain finally walked up to her. "Sorry, Kelly, this is a secure area."

She didn't give a damn. "Paul, can I get some help here?"

He knew better than to think she'd just walk away. "Same old Kelly, fastest scanner in the West. Look, could you give me a few minutes? I'm not even up to speed yet." Kelly had to get a handle on this before everyone was wheeled away. "What do you have so far?" she asked. Kramer told her, "All I know is we've got five bad guys down, one guard and one civvy."

She was shocked. "Five down? And it's officer involved?"

Before he could answer, Vaughn pulled him aside. "Excuse me, Kelly. I'll be right back," said Kramer.

Kelly watched the look on the Captain's face change as Vaughn quietly talked to him and then walked away. From a distance Kramer called out to her, "I'll catch you in a little while. Call my office. I'll get back to you." Kelly knew better. "Your office? Phil? What's the deal? PHIL?"

But it was too late, he'd walked back into the bank and chosen to ignore her. Kelly's eyes followed Detective Vaughn as he left the crime scene and headed toward his unmarked car across the street. She ran to catch up with him and introduced herself. "Daniels, *Chronicle* . . ."

Vaughn threw her an icy smile but said not a word as he kept walking. She persisted anyway: "You mind telling me what the hell is going on here?"

Vaughn came on polite. "Sorry, ma'am, you should have asked the officer in charge."

Kelly thought this guy was a real pain. She said, "I thought I knew most of the plainclothes guys around here. You're a new face." It wasn't going to work; Vaughn kept walking. Again, she tried to get him to open up: "You may not be in charge, but you sure shut Paul Kramer up in a hurry. Who are you? I.A.? Intelligence? Fed?"

Vaughn gave her a very hard look. Kelly was undaunted. "You do have a name, don't you?"

Vaughn stopped before getting in his car. "Please speak to the officer in charge. I'm not going to tell you again."

Kelly was going to push it one way or the other. "Oh? Then what *are* you gonna do?"

Vaughn got in his car, started the motor, and looked up at her standing on the sidewalk. A long moment went by before he said, "Have a nice day." They were his last words as he left her there standing alone.

LIAR'S POKER

The Code Seven Bar was not that big, and between the guys from the S.I.S. and some of the other Friday-night regulars it was full of smoke and loud talk. In the back around the one big table sat Vaughn's unit. At the bar by himself sat Jeff Powers, like a lone wolf.

Larson was, as usual, winning at Liar's Poker. Angel lost another hand. "Shit!" was his first reaction. Larson smiled, which got Angel more riled. "Goddam it, Larson! That's three games in a row."

Larson couldn't have been happier. "You boys ready to play with fifties yet?" he asked. Cusack told him, "Keep laughing, asshole. I'll get you myself on the next hand. Besides, didn't you know, 'rich cops' are two words that never get together."

A couple of the guys looked toward Powers as Larson started to deal again. Angel asked the question. "What's with Powers?" Vaughn responded, "He's finding his balance."

Larson wanted to know what that meant: "What's his fucking problem?" Vaughn told him, "Hey, hot shot, remember *your* first time?"

Angel remembered the first time Larson had killed a perp, and said, "Yeah, cowboy! You were cleaning puke off your boots for a week." They shared a laugh.

Then Vaughn decided he'd better bring Powers back into the fold, and went over to talk to him at the bar. "Feel all right?" he asked.

Powers felt lousy but lied, "Sure, why not?"

Vaughn signaled for another shot from the bartender and said, "We went through some heavy shit today, kid." Powers thought for a second about what he was going to say and said it anyway, "You . . . didn't even try to arrest them."

The bartender put the drink in front of Vaughn, who downed the double in a quick tip of the glass. "You're right. I saw a threat, and I answered it with necessary force."

Powers didn't feel it was that cut-and-dry. "You didn't even identify yourself."

Vaughn smiled. "You did; almost got you capped."

Vaughn was right about that, but Powers felt there was more. "I don't want to have to cover for you. Not after all this time," Powers muttered.

Vaughn shrugged. "What? Should I have waited until after they had a hostage? Or, just until they blew away the guard?"

Powers downed his own drink. He knew Vaughn had had no choice. "Yeah. Yeah, you're right. I just didn't expect to kill them all."

Vaughn just smiled. He put his arm around Powers and walked him back to the table, saying, "That's the job, right? Making the tough calls? You'll get used to it. C'mon, have a drink with the team. They may look like scumbags but they're the best there is. And, they'll be watching your back." They sat down with the others.

"He's right, amigo. Better be nice to us!" said Angel.

Powers was still unsteady, but he smiled anyway. He knew it was baptism by fire with this group. No one had forced him to join. He was honored to be a part of

104

the S.I.S., even if this first assignment had nearly gotten him killed. "Next round's on me," he said to the waitress.

"Make it a beer," said Vaughn.

"A fuckin' ton of it!" chimed in Angel.

It felt right, they were a team, a deadly one at that, but a team nonetheless.

Outside the Code Seven, Kelly was doing her own surveillance. She had followed her instincts and figured Vaughn would go back to police headquarters: Parker Center. She felt Vaughn had come on much too strong to be just some undercover guy working out of a district station. And, when Dan left headquarters after filing his report, Kelly had followed him to the Code Seven, where she'd been sitting outside for nearly three hours now, waiting for him to exit.

What Kelly didn't expect was to see the whole unit stumble out, loaded to the gills--including Jeff. She slid lower in her seat and watched as Angel tripped coming out the door. He had to be helped up off the sidewalk by his friends. She watched Jeff and Dan Vaughn walk down to their cars together. There was nothing more she needed to know.

Kelly raced home to be there before Jeff arrived, but he didn't show up for another two hours. He'd been walking along the Venice canals for some time, deep in thought, before he'd decided to come in. She saw him standing on the small bridge behind their house, and put a robe on, deciding it was okay to go out and meet him. She couldn't wait any longer.

The evening was lit by a full moon that cast reflections of the houses onto the canal water. It seemed especially quiet compared to the rest of the day.

Jeff heard the patio door of their place slide open and watched Kelly hurry over to him. He was surprised she was still up. "You're up late. Working on a story?"

She didn't answer. He tried to hug her, but felt her resist.

Kelly wasn't one for small talk. "Who's that guy you came out of the bar with?" she asked.

Before he could catch himself, he answered, "That's Dan Vaughn . . . How do you know?"

Kelly pressed on, "I met him at the bank shooting today."

Powers pulled away to get a look at her face. He turned and tossed a few stones into the water below, refusing to look at her. The more he thought about her last few words, the less he wanted to talk at all. He started walking back toward the house.

Kelly knew she had hit a raw nerve and followed, even more insistent. He hadn't reached the door when she started up again: "He walked around the crime scene like he owned the place. He shut down one of my best department sources, and then wouldn't even tell me his name."

Powers had had enough. "You're spying on me?"

"No, I'm spying on Vaughn. But I want to know how you're connected to him."

She'd really crossed the line this time—the one they'd promised never to touch. "You're starting to sound an awful lot like a reporter," he said. Kelly had to go on: "I am a reporter."

Jeff's feelings were a jumble of mixed emotions. "Not with me, remember? Nothing leaves the room, right?" She knew this was going to get worse. "Something just came into the room, Jeff. Seven victims. No arrests, just seven body bags . . ."

He got defensive, he had a right to be. "Five perpetrators. Get your facts straight."

Kelly felt that was only part of it; she was angry. "And your drinking buddy wants to keep a lid on it." She waited for Jeff's response, and there was none. "If *I* don't ask, the paper will just send someone else to do it."

Jeff didn't care. "Let them! Then I can tell the reporter to go to hell without screwing up my life."

They entered the house, but there was no place for either of them to hide. "Jeff, come on . . ." she finally pleaded.

It was beyond the talking stage as far as he was concerned. "I have an early briefing. I'll crash on the couch--okay?"

There wasn't really anything more she could say and she knew it. "Okay, okay . . ." she said as she watched him disappear into the den, slamming the door between them.

ROBERTO TORRES

Some perps come from broken homes, or have had parents who abused them, or were surrounded by the wrong people during a time when they were most impressionable. Generally, when you examine the life of a thief, or of a killer for that matter, you find a history of negative influences that help explain their abhorrent behavior and what made them the person they are today.

Roberto Torres was an exception. There were no excuses. He came from a loving family in which the parents both worked hard to give him and his brothers and sisters a better life than most of their neighbors provided in the barrio.

His mother talked the nuns into letting Roberto into a private Catholic school on a scholarship based on need. His father worked two shifts, desperately trying to find the extra money so that little Roberto could have the clothes and the books he needed.

In the end, none of it made any difference. You might as well say Roberto was born under the wrong star. He didn't care about his family, he resented their poverty, he disdained his cultural heritage, and had little or no respect for the Church or its values. As a kid, he enjoyed stealing little things from his mother's purse, or off the desk of a nun at school, or out of the locker of a so-called friend. They owed it to him, all of them, he believed.

When he got caught, Roberto blamed himself for

"making a mistake": the mistake of getting caught, not of doing something wrong. And then, he pretended to be sorry. He wasn't sorry--ever. They deserved to be conned or lied to. He felt that if you could get away with it, then it was the other person's fault for being too stupid to recognize him for what he was: a liar, a cheat, and ultimately a murderer and rapist.

Captain Shafer walked briskly into a packed and noisy S.I.S. briefing room. Vaughn's squad and other support Detectives were engaged in animated conversations, but quickly silenced themselves when he entered.

Dominating the front of the room was the large, rear-screen projection mat. It was primed and held steady a video freeze frame of Roberto Torres and his friends buying lunch at a small street-side joint in their barrio neighborhood.

As usual, Shafer opened the briefing without any wasted words: "Old business: I.A. and O.I.S. have ruled that the bank shooting was clean. There will be no further inquiries." There was an audible sigh of relief from the men. He went on, "I also understand from the hospital that Detective Lloyd will be okay, but he may not be returning, as he is considering retirement." No one was surprised by that decision.

Shafer continued, "It's a good time to mention that stress is as real a hazard in this job as gunfire. Don't macho it out; if you feel uptight, come see me. The Department can help. And finally, concluding old business: Detective Sergeant Jeff Powers is now officially partnered with Dan Vaughn, on a permanent basis."

There was a "welcoming" reaction from the men around Powers. He was in.

"All right, gentlemen, new business. . . . After a brief eighteen-month vacation at the taxpayers' expense, Roberto Torres, Raymond Chavez, and Luis Herrera have been returned to the streets of L.A."

Again, the shifting in their seats, and a barely audible groan from Vaughn's squad indicated that they knew where the Captain was heading.

"Obviously," he said, "you all remember Torres. . . . Well, it seems we made a few mistakes the last time we took him down."

Cusack spoke without thinking. "Yeah, we left him breathing." The laughter in the room was no joke to the Captain. "Cusack, the wrong person hears a remark like that, and the section could be all done. We aren't some third-world death squad in here. Secure that crap."

An aide flicked off the lights and hit the projection switch. On the big screen in front of them, photos of Torres, Chavez, and Herrera flashed on one after the other: mug shots and single-framed long-lens surveillance pictures. These were three tough, angry-looking Latinos in their early twenties.

Shafer got to the point. "Gentlemen, what we have here are three serial rapists, specializing in ambushing young girls in their van. We know they rape. They *brag* about it in jail! But the best we've gotten them on is battery, because we've never caught them in the act. The victims were too scared to testify, so, Misters, Torres, Chavez, and Herrera are out again, looking for some fun. Let's give them more than they bargained for."

There was a sound of agreement from the squad. The lights were flipped on. Shafer finished up: "All right. Dismissed."

Most of the men had left the room when Shafer motioned for Powers and Vaughn to come over because he wanted to talk. He started with Jeff. "Vaughn said you're dating a reporter?"

Powers was caught off-guard but kept it cool. "Don't worry, Cap. We don't talk shop."

Shafer wasn't impressed. "I don't like it. Remember . . . we keep a low profile around here." Powers was concerned. "Yes, sir," he acknowledged. Vaughn tried to lighten the situation: "Don't worry about him, Cap. He won't shit where he eats."

Shafer cracked a small smile that quickly faded. "Vaughn, I *want* Torres and his crew. I've got a daughter of my own. When you take 'em down this time, make it stick."

Vaughn didn't need any encouragement on this one; he'd liked what he was told. "Loud and clear, Cap."

Shafer left the room; he'd made his point.

THE LAST RAPE

Cruising slowly down Broadway in the barrio with Torres at the wheel, Raymond Chavez, and Luis Herrera passed a crack pipe and a joint between each other. It was 10:30 P.M., and the three rapists surveyed every women they passed. Each was a prospective victim, each was looked over for her potential to please all three men.

"There's some *puta*, eh?" asked Torres.

Chazez took a deep drag on the glass crack pipe, and disagreed: "*Chinga*, she's too old. We need something fresh."

They laughed and kept driving. Herrera finished the last of the joint and grabbed the pipe away from Chavez. "Don't be such a pig with the crack, man!"

Torres turned the music up on the radio; he liked the rap song.

Nearly two blocks behind them, Powers used a special pair of military high-powered night-vision binoculars to see what was going on. Vaughn was driving.

"These guys smoke crack like it was a sport," said Powers. Vaughn didn't care about the crack. "Loose change. Like the Cap said, we take these pricks down, and we make it stick."

Powers watched intently as Torres' van continued through the barrio and slowed as it passed a local Spanish-language theater that was closing. In the van all three of them eyed a young theater employee as she said good night to her friends and started walking alone down the street.

Torres was ripped. "I like her ass, man. I wanna fuck this one."

Chavez was ready to take her. "Nice tits, man, this is the one."

Torres stepped on the gas and drove ahead of her a hundred feet to a small parking lot set between two buildings. He turned into it and parked the van. The lights on the van went out and it blended into the shadows. The van was like a dark, hidden animal, waiting for prey.

Down the street, Rosa, a pretty Hispanic girl, walked closer to the alley, heading right for the van.

Farther up the street, Angel sat in his car, watching everything. He picked up the mic. "Latino girl, heading down the street."

Rosa walked through the shadows, oblivious to the threat ahead of her. Torres hopped out of the van and waited beside it. As she passed the van, he stepped out from the shadows, startling her. "Don't be scared, baby, I'm just out selling some jewelry I got. You know, something nice for you or your mother."

Rosa hurried a little to get past him, but he was blocking her way. He stayed close to the back of the van.

"C'mon, I got some jewelry for sale. You want some? I'll let you pick a piece free if you bring your mama to buy some." Torres opened the van door. "C'mon, just look. It's real pretty."

She was hooked. She took one step over to the back of the van and, suddenly, hands shot out from the darkness and yanked her inside.

Vaughn and Powers had watched the whole setup from across the street, where they'd parked. They watched as Rosa tried to struggle free and as Torres grabbed her roughly from behind and literally threw her into the van. He jumped in and slammed the door shut behind them.

Powers drew his gun and opened his car door. Vaughn grabbed him by the shoulder and ordered him, "Not yet."

Powers was stunned. "What?"

Vaughn calmly said it again. "We wait. I want him on felony rape, air-tight."

Down the block, Angel gripped his gun nervously. He picked up the mic. "I don't like this. He's fucking with a barrio girl."

Larson and Cusack were already in position and hidden behind a concrete piller. Cusack spoke into the portable radio mic: "What do you care about a barrio girl, you're Cuban, you dumb shit." Angel replied, "Someday I'll explain it to you, you Polack. I just think Vaughn should call it, *like now*."

In the van, a brown, muscular hand clamped over Rosa's mouth. Torres grinned, then ripped her skirt above her waist, exposing her white panties. She tried to struggle free but was held in place by Chavez and Herrera. Torres told her, "It's gonna be real good, honey. You bitches always gotta learn the hard way . . ." He ripped off the top of her dress, exposing her bra. Maybe she was fifteen. Maybe.

Rosa pleaded for her life, "Please, God . . . Don't do this!" Torres enjoyed seeing her cry, because, he thought, there was no pain that would ever match his own. "Don't worry, baby. You're gonna thank me when it's over!"

Rosa was a virgin, she was more than scared, she prayed aloud, "Dear Jesus ... please don't let this happen..." She was so scared she started to faint, but Chavez and Herrera began to fondle her as Torres fumbled with his pants. Herrera gripped her throat when she tried to scream. Rosa gasped for air.

Then Torres got mad. He told them both, "What am I, a free show? Get the fuck out and wait your turn." Chavez and Herrera reluctantly did what they were told, hopping out of the van while slamming the door behind them. They stood next to it like vultures awaiting their turn.

Across the street, Powers was too preoccupied with Vaughn to notice they'd gotten out. He tugged at Vaughn's hand, but Vaughn held him.

Then Powers wouldn't be held any longer, he'd had it. "Let go! Let's move!"

Vaughn got irritated. "Not yet, dammit!"

Powers was freaked out, to say the least. "I'm not just going to sit here and let this go down!" He forcefully removed Vaughn's hand and got out of their car.

Vaughn was pissed. "Powers, godammit!"

Jeff turned back to him as he cocked the chamber on his gun and said, "What are you gonna do, boss? Write me up for stopping a rape?" Powers turned and ran for the van.

Vaughn punched the dashboard out of frustration. He picked up the mic. "All units, move in!"

Herrera pulled a pistol from his waist when he saw Powers running their way. He saw the gun in Powers' hand and took aim. When Powers heard the sound of gunfire, he dove the last ten feet behind an alley dumpster as two shots barely missed him, ricocheting off the metal trash container. Then he popped up and fired back.

Herrera and Chavez hid behind the van for a moment. Then both of them stepped out and fired their weapons. Powers ducked low as rounds slammed into the concrete wall behind him.

Angel slapped the magnetic light on the roof of the car. He started the engine and gunned it away from the curb, wheeling it down the alley behind them all. He skidded the car sideways to a stop, to use as a shield. Herrera turned the other way and fired at him, exploding the glass in the door above his head.

Larson and Cusack couldn't believe Powers had jumped them all. "What's he doing?" asked Cusack. Larson pumped a round into his shotgun and answered, "Fucking showboat! He's movin' ahead of us, with no backup!"

They moved out from behind the pillar and ran with Vaughn across the street after Powers. Moving quickly, they saw Powers fire again, keeping the two Chicanos pinned down.

With Larson and Cusack at Vaughn's side, the three of them walked slowly into the parking lot, waiting for the perps to show themselves. Boldly, they moved one step after another--as if they were a posse from an old Western advancing on the killers without fear. And when Herrera and Chavez made their move from behind the van, they didn't expect Powers to have three partners with shotguns and an automatic AK-47 assault rifle facing them down. They were caught in a crossfire the moment Angel popped his head up and started shooting.

Chavez was the first to get wasted. He took a series of rounds to the chest and face that made his body gyrate from the impact. Angel's hits to his back pushed him forward while shotgun blasts to his chest pushed him the other way. Back and forth he rocked, until he ended up looking like a butchered piece of meat.

Herrera's gun jammed and he struggled with the firing pin until it was his turn. Vaughn hit him three times in one arm, almost tearing it off. This spun him around to face Angel, who dropped him with one round through the heart. He fell right next to his buddy.

The shots had stopped for only a moment when both van doors exploded open and Torres jumped out with his gun to Rosa's head. He held her tightly, using her partially clad body as a shield. The crack was exploding his head, he was crazy. "Back off, you assholes," he screamed. "I'm warning you! I'll waste her."

Powers held his gun with both hands, but not steady enough to know for sure he would hit Torres and not Rosa if he fired. "You're not going anywhere with the girl. Let her go," Powers told him.

But Torres didn't care what the cop said. "Man, I'll do her! Don't fuck with me!"

Powers felt this guy was crazy enough to do anything. "Look at me, homeboy ... I'm trying to save you," Powers yelled. "You got cops all around you. You pull that trigger, your mama won't recognize you in the morgue."

Torres looked down at what was left of his two

homeboys and felt a tinge of fear. He glanced around, looking at the squad.

Behind Powers, Vaughn walked slowly forward. He flicked on the laser sight on his AK-47 and a red beam of light slowly rose up off the ground and traveled up Torres' frame.

Powers tried again. "Let her go, and put the heat down, easy. Better to live than to die."

Torres hesitated; he wasn't used to making decisions. His finger moved nervously on the trigger.

Vaughn raised his AK-47 a little higher. The red laser dot snaked up the side of Torres' neck and face until it came to rest right between the Latino's eyes. The barrio punk knew they weren't going to let him go. He eased his finger back off the trigger and very, very slowly started to lower the nozzle aimed at Rosa's head. Then, BLAAM!—Torres' head snapped back from the impact of Vaughn's rifle shot. His body slumped backwards and his finger jerked the trigger, spasmodically. The gun went off, killing Rosa instantly, in a bloody splash. Their bodies fell in a pile next to the two others already dead on the ground.

Powers couldn't believe his eyes. He stepped forward and in one motion turned and cold-cocked Vaughn, knocking him off his feet. Vaughn instantly recovered, a murderous look on his face.

Powers was livid. "I had him, Vaughn! I HAD HIM! Why the fuck did you do that!?"

Vaughn ran his hand over his bleeding lip and told him, "I made a judgment in a hostage situation. That's my job. If you had followed orders, it wouldn't have happened."

Powers didn't buy it, any of it, and said so: "BUT HE KILLED THE GIRL. *You* killed her!"

Vaughn pushed Powers back. He'd had enough. "You think I don't know that?"

It had all been said, they just glared at each other for a moment.

Cusack turned toward the bodies. "Hey, he saved the state the price of feeding that bastard, and his two friends," he said to Powers. "And he won't be raping little girls anymore."

Powers was fed up. He pointed to Rosa. "Especially that one."

That did it for Vaughn. "You saying something, Jeff? You saying it wasn't righteous? He had a fucking gun to the girl's head.I can handle anything I.A. wants to throw at us."

Powers was amazed at how fast Vaughn was covering for himself and the squad. "That's not the fucking point! This isn't about I.A.!" he said.

Sirens in the background were fast approaching. Larson knew they had to rap it up. "Enough of this," he muttered. "We don't need to discuss this in front of the whole fucking city, do we?" Into the alley now poured a half-dozen units, including an ambulance and a TV news van. All of the men looked up to see the reporter and her crew quickly getting ready to shoot some tape. Vaughn wasn't about to let that happen.

"Christ. Just what we need. I'll finish with you later," he told Powers.

Vaughn walked over to the TV crew, while Angel took Powers aside. "What's with you, amigo? You wanna get cut from the team? I *like* you. Be smart. That way you'll stick around."

Powers looked at Angel and realized that, first and last, these guys were a team . . . no matter what happened.

DEADLINES

Kelly was working in her cubicle at the paper. She was surrounded by a hundred others in an office that looked like organized chaos because all of them worked to a deadline. Up and down the aisles, copy boys, ad salesmen, and support staff scurried--all seemingly in a rush. It didn't phase Kelly: she was fired up.

Her agitated hands twisted the telephone cord as she waited impatiently while someone kept her on hold. When they answered again, she snarled: "I've called them *already*! They sent me to *you*! You mean to tell me you don't even know where your own officers are assigned?" She didn't like his next answer either, and told him, "I'll shout if I damn well want to!"

WHAM! She slammed the phone down, knocking over her coffee.

Max Alvarez, her editor, was walking by and figured it must be a good story to get her this riled. He teased her, "Caffeine bothering you, Kel?"

She didn't laugh. "I'm not in the mood, Max. I got this spooky cop named Vaughn stone walling me on a major shooting, and no one will give me a thing! L.A.P.D. won't even tell me where he's assigned."

Max had an idea. "If you can't ask the shooters, why not ask the guys who got shot?"

Kelly's frustration bubbled over. "They're dead, Max. That's the point. I *notice* these things. That's why I'm a reporter."

Max knew better. "Yeah, and dead people go to the

morgue, where a lot of people look 'em over. I notice things, too; that's why I'm the editor."

Kelly sat back in her chair, taken aback by the simplicity of his suggestion. "The morgue! Damn, it was looking me right in the face. Thanks, Max."

He smiled and shook his head in amazement. He walked back to his office, leaving her scrambling to grab her things and leave.

In the days and nights that had followed the Torres rape, Kelly and Jeff had been on different schedules and, as luck would have it, simply never crossed paths. For Jeff Powers, it had been a time of new briefings, surveillance training, and a lot of introspective hindsight about the events that took place that night in the alley. He wondered what kind of effect years of this work had had on the other men in the S.I.S. He knew the men were friends off-duty and on, and he couldn't detect any special differences among them that separated them mentally from other Detectives and special units in general. He also knew that cops were all just one color: blue. It was a phenomenon that was universal among all police forces. This was a job that you chose. That you had wanted to do from the time you were in your teens or--for a lot of men and women--before that. It was a job that often passed on from generation to generation.

Powers knew that although much had been written and described about the life of a cop, no civilian could ever really understand how it felt to *be* one. Ironically, it was more of a problem for a cop to try and understand how a civilian really felt, because once you had dedicated yourself to law enforcement, you never really would think again like an ordinary citizen. He also knew this was a problem most large police forces had acknowledged, and tried to correct through programs designed to keep your average street cop in tune with the people. But the truth was, the real world didn't give a shit about cops, and the cops had finally conceded that it just wasn't possible to get civilians to understand their day-to-day problems.

And so, for Jeff Powers, the men of the S.I.S. represented one of the first serious actions a police department had ever taken to really fight crime in an aggressive way, and do it with a win-the-war mentality. They were envied by their peers for their ability to use any means available to shut down repeat offenders. They were respected by other cops on the street, by those same men and women who often, themselves, took incredible risks to protect and serve people--who very often hated them.

When you put it all together, Jeff Powers knew from the day his father was killed that he wanted to be doing exactly what he was doing today. But something was bothering him, something deep within himself. . . . It was like a nagging ache somewhere within, which could not be pinpointed, which was only felt for a moment but which wouldn't let him forget it was there. Something about Vaughn and the way he worked. Something that was taking him, Powers, to a place he wasn't sure he wanted to discover. It was a like a deep, dark secret hidden away from everyone--except, probably, Captain Shafer.

Shafer had been around a long time. Long enough to have a sixth sense about such things. It was what made him a leader among leaders. It wasn't something you learned in school, it was a quality that came from a lot of time and experience. It was a quality that now told Shafer it was time to have a little talk with Jeff Powers.

Shafer had his own way of doing things, and today was another example. He'd asked Powers and Vaughn to meet him in Echo Park, a sanctuary bordering east L.A. and the barrio. It was heavily patrolled by enough black-and-whites that women felt safe strolling their babies around the small man-made lake. It had once been a place where the local barrio kids shot the ducks and swans for target practice. However, the local precinct had finally put a stop to that.

At one end of the park, you could sit on a bench and lazily spend an afternoon reading a book, or enjoy a hot dog from a local pushcart vender. It was here that Shafer decided to have a little chat with his boys, and not in the S.I.S. concrete bunker three floors below the city streets at Parker Center.

As Shafer bit into a hot dog, he walked with the two of them saying nothing. Powers was already beginning to feel a little uneasy as he waited for Vaughn's boss to speak. He didn't have to wait too long before Shafer asked, "What the fuck happened out there! The press is saying you 'watched a rape.' You wanna tell me about it?"

Vaughn answered as usual, in a very calm and deliberate manner. "Nothing to tell: We followed the perps, they snatched the girl, and we moved in. They heard us, and Torres took a hostage. He freaked, and wasted her. We took 'em all down resisting. End of story."

Shafer, suspecting more, asked Powers: "Is that the way you see it?"

Powers gave Vaughn a look.

Shafer wasn't into looks, he was into answers, and he said, "Powers, you're living up to your rep. The City Council is going to grill you like top sirloin. I've worked too many years to see this squad burned by some political jerk-off." Finishing the last of his hot dog, he continued, "You know what a 'good soldier' is?"

Powers had an educated guess. "Sure. A guy who doesn't break ranks."

Shafer wasn't so sure, and he walked off down another path alone. He turned back to Powers with one last thought: "Try *being* one. You'll last longer."

Powers and Vaughn watched him move away. They stood alone near the water's edge. Jeff knew the conversation wasn't over. Vaughn spoke first.

"Don't sweat the City Council. You'll do the right thing." Vaughn's smile was an attempt to close the matter and get the affirmation from Powers that he had to have. He didn't get it.

Powers said, "I told you, I'm done covering for you."

Vaughn then asked him the real question: "What are you going to tell the Council?"

The look between them gave nothing away. Powers gave him the truth; he thought it the best path to follow. "I wish the fuck I knew! How can you just sit in the car and watch crimes go down, Dan? What about

'TO PROTECT AND SERVE'?''

Vaughn stepped closer, to make his point. "If there was no S.I.S., the crimes would happen anyway."

Powers didn't think Vaughn was getting *his* point. "We watched a little girl get raped, man. I can't fucking hang with that."

Vaughn turned his head and looked over the lake to the city beyond before he spoke again. "That little girl would've been raped and killed anyway. I don't know, Jeff, maybe I lose it sometimes. Sheila left me about a month ago. Said she couldn't live with what I do. Maybe I jumped the gun, but those three fuckers will never hurt anyone else again.

"Would you'd like it better if Torres had gotten away? I took the shot. Maybe it was wrong. And I have to live with it. That's the job."

Powers tried to look beyond Dan's eyes. The tone in his friend's voice and his whole demeanor seemed as real as you could get. Powers was beginning to understand.

Vaughn could tell; he walked past him and patted him on the shoulder. "You'll do good, kid. I trust you. . . . See you in the Council Room, partner."

Powers watched him walk away. Inside, he felt the same ache that he'd known before. The pain he just couldn't put his finger on.

Kelly walked into a place where no one seemed to feel any pain . . . at least not anymore: the City Morgue.

As usual, the place appeared to be in complete chaos. Bodies lined the halls on gurneys, some having dripped what looked like their last few pints onto the tiled floor. White-coated attendants hustled around with clipboards full of paperwork.

She breezed in, not even having to show her Press Pass, and was astounded by the pace and overload of the place. An attendant shoved a gurney with an uncovered corpse right in front of her, slamming it against the wall. For a second she thought the stiff was going to drop to the floor but then noticed he was strapped down. But it was sloppy parking, to say the least. The same attendant yanked open a closet for some forms, which also revealed several white lab coats hanging inside. He called out to a co-worker, "Hey, Tom! We're out of body bags! Let's get some blankets for the meat!"

Turning to her, he winked an eye.

Kelly tried to smile, but she didn't laugh. Her own sense of humor had evaporated thirty seconds before, when she'd walked through the door.

She now watched both attendants leave, and opened the closet again. She took one of the coats and put it on, grabbing a clipboard as a prop. Then she walked down the hallway into the dissection room at the end.

Inside, Dr. Roseman, the County Coroner for Los Angeles, was standing over a body on a slab finishing his report. A voice-activated mic hung from the ceiling over the body.

When Kelly stepped into the room, she was overcome by the foulest-smelling odor she would ever come to know. Roseman saw the contorted look on her face as she tried to cover her nose. He smiled and asked, "You new here?"

Kelly surmised that the doctor had her pegged for a

med student, but she couldn't hold her breath another second. She did her best not to throw up, answering him, "Does it show?"

Dr. Roseman laughed. "Only the new ones want to puke. Doesn't smell like medical school, does it? What do you need?"

Kelly went with the flow. "We've lost the paperwork on Torres. Gunshot wound."

Roseman chuckled to himself. "You mean Vaughn gunshot wound. Multiple shots, close-range. If the poor S.O.B. had lived, he'd have died from lead poisoning."

Kelly thought this guy had the strangest sense of humor of all of them. She attempted a smile. "'Vaughn Gunshot'? Sounds like a German injury."

Roseman liked this intern. "Good! You've got a sense of humor." He pointed to the corpses around them. "We've got a pretty tough audience. Vaughn is the shooter. We get his work all the time. I hear they save the real bad guys for the S.I.S. Of course, they all look the same to me."

Kelly began scribbling notes on her clipboard. She couldn't believe her luck. "S.I.S.? That's . . ."

He told her, "Special Investigation Section. So what else do you need?" He pointed to the body behind them, a fully opened cadaver. "Over here, the cause is multiple-gunshot trauma, all in the back-- Oh, hell, let me finish here. I'll get my tape."

Kelly felt she had to push on this one. "What's the S.I.S. for?"

She'd pushed too far. Roseman wondered what the hell she was driving at. "What are you talking about?"

he questioned. "The S.I.S. What's its *assignment*?" Dr. Roseman changed his attitude completely. Who the hell was she to be asking these kinds of questions? He stepped toward her and she automatically started to back out of the room. "Why do you . . . ?" And then he suddenly realized she wasn't any med student at all.

"Who are you?" he demanded.

Kelly turned on her heel and on the way out the door said, "Thanks, Doc, I'll have another look for the report."

Her impromptu interview was over and she walked quickly down the hall. Dr. Roseman dropped the lower intestine he held in his hand and pursued her out the door. As Kelly passed one of the attendants, she handed him the clipboard but took the notes she had scribbled on a piece of paper. "Here, I think this is yours," she whispered. Dr. Roseman was not far behind, but there were so many bodies being wheeled in at the time that he lost her in the crowd.

It took Kelly several hours to recover. She went straight home, took the longest shower of her life, changed clothes, and put her old ones in a large zip-tight plastic bag. On the way back to her office she dropped them at the cleaners and specifically told them to be sure they were deodorized and dry-cleaned.

Once back at the *Chronicle*, she went to one of the researcher's desks and turned on the big computer screen they worked at. She went into the newspaper's giant data base and punched up the three letters she was most curious about: S.I.S.

The high-speed computer blew through millions upon millions of words in its search. In a matter of minutes it had worked its way through twenty-five years of police stories, when it finally came up with the two words she didn't expect: "Not Found."

She couldn't believe it, she didn't want to believe it. She tried it one more time, using the full name, "SPECIAL INVESTIGATION SECTION." Again, the computer displayed the same two words: "Not Found."

Kelly was exasperated; then she got another idea and typed it in quickly: "MULTIPLE GUNSHOT WOUNDS . . . VAUGHN." Within seconds, the first story came up on the screen, including a crime scene photo of two bloody corpses in front of a bank. Kelly peered at the screen, reading the copy. It was the story of an aborted bank robbery: Two blacks, one male, one female, had robbed a Sherman Oaks bank. They had parked their car in the alley behind it and left through an emergency exit. In the alley waiting for them were what she judged correctly must have been members of the S.I.S. unit.

The man had been hit first, apparently by five of the S.I.S. men at the same time. The article went on to report that the coroner listed nearly forty entry wounds, all in the back. The woman had been shot just once, wounded in the arm, and had then surrendered. Vaughn's name figured prominently in the story.

She hit the "search" button again and again. Story after story involving multiple-gunshot wounds and Vaughn appeared on the screen. Picture after picture of shattered, bloody bodies in cars, or lying on the pavement.

Kelly had struck home and was totally caught up in what she had found. Again, Vaughn's name came up, but this time it was coupled with a "Detective Larson." She used Larson's name to cross-check and came up with several other stories--but none of them ever mentioned the name or the three initials indicating it had been an S.I.S. operation. She felt in her heart that they were all S.I.S. operations, but somehow the police always kept the name of the special unit out of the papers. Furthermore, the stories never tied it all together or disclosed the recurring nature of the unit's business. For more than twenty years, the S.I.S. had never appeared to raise the suspicions of the press.

For over two hours she filtered through the stories, taking names, dates, and . . . a body count.

Some of the stories had grizzly photos. One in particular showed a picture of three Chinese gang members who had been gunned to death in their car, paired with a photo of a fireman hosing the blood off the street.

A third name, "Cusack," came up and she added it to the others. Altogether, she had over thirty stories involving the group. The evidence to support its clandestine activities was substantial. She went back through the computer files and began to make printouts of the most startling cases. Finally, she organized the copies and highlighted the names and then put them together in a chronological fashion. She was ready to present all of it to Max, and hurried with the thick folder down to her editor's office.

Max could tell from the determination with which she walked in, without knocking, that Kelly had something going. She dropped the folder on his desk, saying, "Take a look, Max." And, for the next ten minutes he quickly reviewed what she'd put together.

Kelly moved around his desk behind him and started to try to sell him. "They follow the crook, sometimes for weeks, and don't touch him until he does a crime. That's Special Investigation Section, the S.I.S. But they want it air-tight, so sometimes they sit by and watch the crime happen. People have been beaten, terrorized, and the cops have been outside--watching. Look at these . . ." she said.

She held up some of the more lurid pictures and continued to sell him, using pure energy and enthusiasm. She continued, "More than half the time, they end up in shootings, and statistically they have the highest percentage of 'kills' of any police unit in the city, including SWAT. Some of the dead are shot in the back, with multiple rounds."

Max was edgy; he moved around in his seat uncomfortably. He didn't like people leading him to the point. It was either there in front of him or it didn't work. He was frustrated and said so: "Pretend I run a newspaper, and want to hear the *short* answer."

Kelly was losing him and she knew it, so she went for the Page One headline and told him, "They're a death squad. An officially sanctioned hit team. They target crooks, and wait until they can kill the bad guys with impunity."

Max didn't like it. "We're not running a cheap tabloid, Kelly. I need facts, not suppositions. What you're telling me is a real mouthful."

She was desperate now. "Nothing else makes sense. They're ultra-secret, nobody in the L.A.P.D. will talk about them, and they have killed more perps per officer than any other squad." She was out of ammo, and pleaded, "You gotta run this Max. This is Page One material."

Max leaned back in his chair and tossed a photo back on the desk. "Okay, I'll run it . . ."

Kelly felt like doing a back flip. "GREAT!"

But Max wasn't finished. ". . . when you get a corroborating source on record. A person inside the Department. Someone I can point to when Legal Affairs comes to visit me."

Kelly's heart skipped a beat. "But . . ." was all she could utter.

Max was not about to go off the deep end without a little water in the pool below. He explained: "I'm supposed to accuse the L.A.P.D. of assassination—with no backup? What would *you* do in my shoes?"

Kelly didn't have to think it about it very long. She knew it wouldn't fly without another source. She glumly gathered the papers off his desk and started to walk out. But she turned in his doorway, knowing he was right but also knowing she wasn't wrong. "I'd probably chicken-out, too, Max."

Max turned in his seat, not wanting to confront her anymore, but he thought to himself that this was the same old Kelly, the one who someday soon he'd either promote or fire.

Kelly was more than let down and didn't figure she'd be much good at the office for the rest of the day. She drove home thinking about it all, over and over. She knew she shouldn't have insulted the boss . . . again. She knew it was going to be tough, if not impossible, to get what she needed. And she also knew she was on to a story that had incredible possibilities if she could verify it.

She pulled up to their house in Venice and for the first time in a week saw Jeff's Jeep parked in front of it. At least she could finally sit down with him for a few minutes and try to untangle their relationship.

Jeff was in the bedroom and heard her pull into the garage below. He didn't stop from putting his gear together, or checking his gun. He was on his way out again, and paused only for a moment in the kitchen to get a Coke out of the fridge. As he popped the lid, he looked at the notes she'd been leaving him, tacked up all over the door: a row of "Dear Jeff's"—each note more frustrated than the last. . . . "Call me," "Where are You?", "I miss you", and the last: "TALK TO ME, JEFF."

Jeff didn't wait for her to come in; he walked out the front door as she came in through the kitchen. She called to him, "Jeff? JEFF?" and then heard the sound of his Jeep driving away from the house. She looked at the notes she'd left all over the fridge door and began to take them down one by one.

The next day found Jeff and the rest of Vaughn's squad in a face-off with a dozen members of the City Council. In a closed-door session, Vaughn stood behind a podium on one side of a wooden railing that extended all the way across the City Hall hearing room. In a half-circle of chairs opposite Vaughn sat the entire City Council, led by Charles Allen. At the far end of this racially mixed and diverse group sat

Joe Taylor, a well-groomed black man in his late forties.

All twelve members of the Council listened attentively to Detective Vaughn as he talked them through the Torres rape and told them, "They took a hostage. All of them were high on crack; anything could've happened. Torres shot the hostage, and I opened fire before he shot anyone else. I just wish I had shot earlier. I might have saved that young girl."

Powers listened with a stony face. He looked at the floor, then the ceiling; he tried hard not to give away how uncomfortable he felt.

Councilman Allen was the first to speak, "Thank you, Detective. We all understand how difficult it must be for you to go over—"

Councilman Taylor interrupted him. He couldn't stand the bullshit and especially Allen. "Ask his partner, *Powers*! Is that the way it went, Detective Powers?"

Allen didn't like being talked over by anyone, especially Taylor, and cut him off before anyone else could speak. "Councilman Taylor, address your questions to the Chair!" He turned and looked across the room toward Powers. "Do you agree with Detective Vaughn?"

The room focused on Powers, including Vaughn. This was it. Powers stood up and said slowly, "Yes . . . yes, I agree."

That was enough for Councilman Allen. He wanted to wrap this whole thing up as quickly as possible, and said, "Now, if we're through wasting time, let's move on. We've all seen the squad's arrest record. It's very impressive. How do you do it?" he asked Vaughn.

Taylor cringed in his seat. He really hated Allen for always sucking up to the Police Department.

Vaughn said, "We are the Department's secret weapon against repeat offenders. We follow hardened criminals, keeping them under surveillance until we can catch them in the act. We draw a line in the street, Councilman. We take the worst of the worst off the streets. Period."

Taylor exploded, "Start asking the hard questions!" He looked at Allen and told him, "You're an L.A.P.D. flunky, Allen. Ask them about Powers!" He stood up in his seat and threw his file folder down on the table."He's been on I.A.'s list for years! Brutality, illegal search, weapons violations. . . . He's a dangerous man!"

Before Allen could respond, Powers spoke up. "Yes, sir, I am. I'm a danger to every repeat offender thinking about committing a crime. Criminals make the rules in the streets, not us. We just react. S.I.S. lets us fight back on an even playing field. And, I'll stack my arrest record against anyone's. I get the job done."

Taylor was even more pissed off than before, and started to rise in his seat again. Allen tried to shut him down. "Mr. Taylor, you get out of order one more time, and--"

Taylor stopped him, saying. "You wanna know what's 'out of order'!? Charles Allen running a police inquiry! You're in bed with every police charity this side of Pomona. Everybody knows you're just covering up for the Department!"

Allen had to respond. "Those allegations are without merit, and are completely--"

But Taylor outshouted him, "Then ask the *real* questions. What about Rosa Rodriguez, the child Torres raped while these heroes sat back and watched!"

Allen grabbed the gavel in front of him and started banging, "You are out of order, Councilman! If you do not restrain yourself--"

However, it was too late to stop Taylor, who screamed at them all, "What kind of police officer watches a child get raped!?"

Vaughn stood up casually, and leaned over the table, moving closer to Taylor. The city politician was intimidated, which in this case made perfect sense. Vaughn asked him, "Would you be happy if S.I.S. hadn't been there? Would you rather have had Torres rape someone else's daughter tonight? Maybe yours?"

Taylor was stunned for a moment. Vaughn continued, "I'm sorry about that girl. Very sorry. But until you put on a badge, you don't know what it's like out there. We took down three serial rapists. Three monsters who won't hurt anyone again. So, if you really want to ask the hard questions, Mr. Taylor, ask yourself if you're on the side of crime, or on the side of justice?"

Vaughn returned to his seat slowly. Taylor was shaken. The squad traded smiles. They knew the inquisition was over. They were right.

Outside the Council Chamber doors, Kelly was pacing, along with several other reporters. They had all been kept out of the Chamber by two police guards. Kelly was fed up with the interference and moved toward the doors. She was going in and flashed her police press badge as if it could get her in anywhere. Both cops stopped her. "Look," she argued, "I'm from the *Chronicle*, and—"

The taller of the two shook his head "no," and said, "Miss, I'm sorry. Closed session means everyone. Even the press. This is a personnel hearing, you can't—"

Kelly interrupted. "Personnel? I thought this was a police hearing?"

The second guard answered this time. "Look, we just know what they tell us."

Before she could say anything else, the huge doors burst open and Councilman Allen strode by. She ran after him along with two other reporters. Kelly was the first to speak. "Mr. Allen, was that meeting about the S.I.S.?" Allen picked up the pace, but responded, "Just personnel matters." Kelly attacked again: "Councilman Taylor is saying you're part of the Police Department's Damage Control. Any comment?" He laughed that one off and replied, "Then, you should take that up with Mr. Taylor, shouldn't you?"

Allen disappeared into the busy lunchtime crowd now flooding into the main hallway. She had lost any hope of cracking the guy. But then, she spotted Councilman Taylor, and gave chase, catching him going into an elevator. "Is there any other information you would like our paper to have?" A quick nod to the negative was all she got as the elevator door closed in her face.

It was time to give it up and call it a day, a rotten day. Dejected, she walked out of the building.

A few moments later, following behind everyone else was the S.I.S. squad. They walked together out of the Council Chamber triumphant . . . and laughing.

Vaughn and Powers lagged behind. Powers was looking moody and Vaughn sensed a problem. They walked down the long corridor before Dan got the ball rolling. "Thanks, kid."

Powers answered, "I didn't do it for you." Vaughn twisted this around: "No. You did it for yourself."

Vaughn was trying hard to be warm and sincere. "You protected yourself, and you protected the team. As long as you take care of the team, the team will take care of you. You can count on that." He patted Powers on the back. "Nice going, Jeff."

Vaughn kept walking and caught up with the other S.I.S. members waiting at the bottom of the steps. Powers slowed his step a bit, and watched him go. Inside Powers' gut that same ache was getting to him again, and this time he knew the choice he'd just made was going to hurt him a lot more.

The decisions Jeff Powers had been forced to make over the last few days had put him into a tailspin. They only compounded his personal relationship with Kelly, and, though they had not seen each other in nearly a week, or discussed anything more about his new assignment, he didn't hold out much hope for maintaining a relationship. He'd never thought his work could come between them, and for two years their arrangement and way of living together had been the best thing he had ever experienced.

All the way home, these thoughts crossed his mind, and they repeated themselves again as he packed his bags and prepared to move out. He heard Kelly enter the house and realized these would be their last few minutes together.

She walked through a darkened living room and called out to him, "Jeff. Are you okay?"

He stepped out of the bedroom, but before she could cross the distance between them he picked up his bag and walked toward the front door. "I'm leaving, Kelly. I don't know for how long."

Kelly didn't want to admit to herself what was happening. She mumbled, "G-Going out of town?" He couldn't look at her but had to say it: "No, just out of here. Things are getting . . . complicated."

Kelly still refused to grasp what was really happening. He told her, "You're asking too many questions, okay? It's making my job very hard. It could get dangerous for me. Things are happening, things you wouldn't understand."

Kelly figured it out very fast. "You're wrong. You mean, things like the S.I.S. and the Torres shooting."

Jeff was trying not to get into another argument if he could help it. "No, you *don't* understand. You don't know what you're talking about."

At this point she decided that if this was it, she wasn't letting him off the hook and out the door without his facing the facts. "Jeff, I know you were involved in the bank shooting. I saw your picture. Look me in the eye and tell me I'm wrong."

He looked away. His jaw muscles flexed. "I never asked you to give up anything for me, have I? Well, now I'm asking. Drop the story. Hand it off to someone else! For *me*, Kelly. For *us*."

A long moment passed. Kelly knew what she had to do, and it was for herself, her soul, for her own integrity. Kelly was going to say what was on her mind if it killed her. "Jeff, I can't just give it up . . . !"

Jeff didn't *expect* her to say anything else, of course.

That was why he figured they were both at a dead end. "Yeah," was all he could manage. He moved past her to a chest of drawers in the living room and packed a few more things.

Kelly figured there was no reason for holding back at this point. "You're not a cop anymore, Jeff. You're . . . you're a hit man. You follow criminals and kill them. You watch crimes happen. You let innocent people get hurt. Why? So you can call it a 'righteous shoot'?"

Whether what she said was true or not—and in his mind there was a good deal of doubt—he wasn't going to roll over and play dead. He had pride, and he knew he was a dedicated cop, not a killer. He went for the jugular. "Would you care so much about this . . . if it wasn't a Page One story?"

It was one of those moments in which both sides have said things each will regret for a long time to come, maybe forever. He walked out the door, bags in hand, leaving Kelly with tears cascading down her cheeks.

THE MARK AND BOBBY SHOW

Across the S.I.S. projection screen, a series of video slides showed Bobby Lewis and several of his gang. Bobby was baby-faced and a real surfer type. He was in his early twenties, had long hair and a short goatee. Not a handsome kid but not your average stick-up artist either.

Captain Shafer stood at the podium running the briefing. "Loosen up, gentlemen. This is stamped urgent. We've got two young armed robbers on the streets that have held up five bars in the last three weeks."

Powers arrived late, looking like hell. He slid into his seat and avoided Shafer's eyes. Vaughn gave him a look, but Powers wouldn't give him the time of day.

As Shafer spoke, the video shots on the screen flashed by. He commented on them: "Bobby Lewis and Mark Franklin rob upscale beach hangouts. The champagne-and-Rolex crowd. Usually around happy hour, when the till is full."

The still videos changed into a moving-surveillance video. Mark Franklin came up on the screen, looking more like a young, handsome actor than part of a gang. He was dressed in beach attire and showed a relaxed attitude as he clowned around with his friends.

The guys in the room threw looks at each other, as if this had to be a mistake. But Shafer continued, "We've got a good tip they've moved into the Venice beach area. Our informant says they've made some new friends and are getting ready to push their luck a little more. We've narrowed their next probable down to three Marina bars. Vaughn, I want your boys to stake-out all three locations. It's time we step in and change the odds. Understood?"

Vaughn said it. "Yes, sir, understood."

The Captain hit a button on the podium and the show was over. He told them, "Keep alert, gentlemen. *People are watching on this one.*"

Kelly was sitting at her desk watching the usual hyper-activity of all those around her. She felt more than left out, she felt depressed, and as if she was stuck in sand with no way to move on her story or her relationship with Jeff.

From over her shoulder Max descended like an Angel, dropping a pile of folders onto her desk. Kelly asked, "These are the background clips I asked for?"

Max dead-panned his efforts. "Look at me, I'm an editor, not your copy boy. Your list isn't even current. One of your cops retired." She couldn't figure that out. "What? *Who* retired?"

Max dug through the pile on her desk and pulled out a recent story about Mike Lloyd's stress retirement. Naturally, there was no mention of the S.I.S. Kelly quickly scanned the article, looked up with her first smile of the day, and said, "You just gave me an in-formed source, Max. I could almost kiss you!"

Max liked the offer, grinned, and returned to his desk. Kelly picked up the phone and worked her sources until she had Lloyd's unlisted phone number and then called him.

She was able to find out that Mike Lloyd was on the

edge before he shot and killed Daisy. He was a casualty of the "war," a cop who couldn't take the pressure. A cop who had worked to keep in mental as well as physical shape but in the end had lost the battle. The life he endured would have stressed out most people in a matter of weeks, and, in some cases, minutes. Lloyd was a dedicated professional, and had been close to a twenty-year retirement. He never made it. Kelly knew that when a cop went over the edge, "close" didn't count. She'd been on the city beat long enough to know that within every major police department there were always mental casualties. What she found really surprising was how few there were, given the circumstances. She also knew that when a cop reached the breaking point, he was taken care of by his own.

Though Kelly didn't know his whole story, Lloyd had seen it all, and then some, on the S.I.S.: kidnappers, killers, rapists, child molesters, you name it. He had been involved in numerous shootings and forced to kill four and now five people, including little Daisy. Each one had been an experience he wished had never occurred. And though his most rewarding experiences had been on the S.I.S., he had reached a point where an overriding sense of guilt began to permeate his thinking and he was scared to death it would affect his reactions. He was scared not so much for his own safety but for the safety of his partners on the squad.

Booze, she surmised, had obviously helped keep him in the game. Booze had a way of shrouding the guilt and taking the edge off his nerves. Once he knew that drinking could keep him on the job, it became a bad habit and finally the disease of an alcoholic.

The day the bank shooting went down was like all the others of the past year or so: He got up and killed a pint of vodka before he was in the shower. During the day he went to the john to down a refill. To some degree his problem was known among his peers, but it was tolerated. To be a cop and drink was not unusual, as long as you weren't seen doing it and didn't fall down on the job. Among the rank and file it was tolerated, but if the suits upstairs got wind of it, your ass was out the door. Experienced cops knew the odds worked against their men and that booze might cover a problem for a while, but in the end it would *be* the problem.

Lloyd's last day on the job was the Friday he flipped out at the bank. And now, sitting at home, alone, there was nothing to keep his mind from facing a very tough reality.

Kelly figured that Lloyd couldn't leave a job like the S.I.S. right away and go off and start doing something. In his case, it was not only out of the question, it was impossible; what he really needed was long-term professional help. He had certainly earned it, and it was available, but no one could force him into a program. So, in the end, after twenty years, he was alone, at home, and feeling like shit.

As he sat on a flower-covered couch on the veranda, all around him were the remnants of his life. The place was a fucking mess. In front of him was an old graduation picture of himself in police dress blues. To look at that and then at Lloyd's face was to see an ugly world of difference. As Lloyd peered into the picture, it changed in front of his eyes: It was a shadow, and then another face--the face of Daisy, which stared directly at him with both of her dead eyes wide open.

Lloyd freaked out and threw the frame across the floor, smashing it against the wall. It snapped him back to a reality that looked worse. Lloyd didn't understand, however, and rubbed his head with the excruciating frustration of a man who knows he is losing his grip.

The phone next to him must have rung a half-dozen times before he heard it and picked it up. Lloyd could barely speak. "Yeah?"

On the other end, a woman's voice came through. "Detective Lloyd? This is Kelly Daniels. . . . *L.A. Chronicle*. I'd like to talk to you."

Lloyd didn't get many phone calls. "About what?" he asked. "About the S.I.S." she said.

He knew better. "I can't . . ."

Kelly wouldn't let go. "Do you want more people to die, Mike?" Lloyd knew she was fucking with him. "You got no right . . ." he told her.

Kelly pushed another button. "You're helping them, every day you don't tell the truth."

Lloyd didn't need anyone else to bring him down. "You got no fucking right! I didn't want it to go down that way . . . didn't want her to . . . Aw, Jesus!" Lloyd's eyes started to water, he was breaking down, it was killing him. He slowly dropped the phone onto the hook.

In another part of the city, Powers and Vaughn stood along the sidewalk near the beach on a stakeout. Each was reading part of the paper, ignoring the other.

Powers looked across the street at St. Peter's Bar, and broke the ice when he asked, "You really think these surfer kids are going to start killing people?"

Vaughn didn't look up from his paper but smiled and answered, "*So* . . . now you're talking to me again? For days you've been acting like I stood you up on prom night."

Powers had to laugh. "Fuck you. I just had a lotta shit in my life." Vaughn could read Powers' life pretty well, and teased him, "Girl trouble?"

Powers was surprised Vaughn could pin it down. "Yeah, well, I kinda broke up, sorta."

Vaughn had it all down. "Dumped by the reporter, huh?"

Powers couldn't help but get defensive. "Dumped? *I* was the one who packed!"

Vaughn had him now, and he smiled. "She threw you out!"

Powers tossed the newspaper in the trash. This guy was too much. "Shit. . . . Drop it. Seriously, I mean, I really don't think these kids are killers. Did you read their jacket? They kid around with the victims, tell bad jokes; I don't see them shooting."

Vaughn was too cynical to see it any other way. "Things go wrong. People discover drugs. It happens."

Powers wasn't convinced at all, and wasn't going to make another mistake. "I'm having the prints double-checked. I don't want to tag the wrong guys."

Vaughn didn't see the need. "Prints are great for lawyers in court, kid, but they don't mean shit on the street. We'll know if they're killers--at about the time they try to blow us away." Vaughn didn't want Powers to have any doubts about who was in charge. "You disobey orders today, Jeff, and I'll kick your fucking ass."

He said it as only Vaughn could, with a smile and a deadly charm. Powers gave him a look as if to blow it off, but couldn't help fidgeting with the position of his gun in its holster.

As Kelly parked her car opposite Lloyd's house, she questioned whether she was going too far. She figured she didn't have much to lose, other than a job that made her life complete; a complete mess, that is. Across the street she looked at his small, rundown, shoebox of a home. Not much for a guy with twenty years on the force.

She opened the screen door and saw the front door was ajar, but she knocked anyway. There was no answer. This was no time to be shy and so she carefully stepped into the house.

Empty bottles of Jack Daniels and pizza cartons littered the floor. Some of the furniture was knocked over. It looked as if the place had been ransacked and deserted. She called out, "Hello? Detective Lloyd?"

Kelly started walking through the silent house, tense with apprehension, for something felt wrong. She walked down the hallway leading to the living room and the veranda out back. She had almost reached the end of it when she looked in the mirror on the wall and could see around the corner Mike Lloyd sitting alone on the flower-covered couch against the wall. He was looking right at her.

"The following still photos were made available through the courtesy of the stars and Trimark Pictures. The still photographer for *Extreme Justice* was Joseph D'Alessio."

The S.I.S. squad (L to R): Lloyd, Angel, Vaughn, Larson, and Cusack.

Scott Glenn as Detective Dan Vaughn, head of the S.I.S. unit.

*Lou Diamond Phillips as Detective Jeff Powers, the new man
on the squad.*

Detectives Vaughn and Powers at Captain Shafer's barbeque.

Chelsea Field as Kelly Daniels, the reporter for the Los Angeles Chronical *investigating the bank shootout.*

Yaphet Kotto as S.I.S. Detective Ben Larson.

Ed Lauter as Captain Shafer.

Larson and Angel (Andrew Divoff) at the bank.

Det. Powers faces down the bank robbers.

Kelly arrives at the bank and starts her investigation.

Kelly asks her friend Captain Kramer (Anthony Herrera) for help.

*Kelly (Chelsea Field) confronts Vaughn (Scott Glenn) after the
bank shootout.*

Kelly at her Los Angeles Chronicle *desk tries to figure out the identity of the men within the S.I.S.*

The S.I.S. get together at the Code 7 bar: (L to R) Cusak (William Lucking), Vaughn, Powers, Angel, Larson.

Torres uses the rape victim as a shield from the S.I.S.

The deadly aftermath of the Torres rape scene: Cusak, Larson, Vaughn, and Powers.

Detective Jeff Powers on the steps of City Hall after giving his testimony.

*S.I.S. Detective Dan Vaughn and Detective Jeff Powers at the
St. Mark's stakeout near the beach in Venice, California.*

The St. Mark's stakeout explodes into a chase through the Venice beach area.

Vaughn (Scott Glenn) chases a young robber through the crowds but can't get a clear shot.

Powers (Lou Diamond Phillips) is about to run into trouble when he's surprised by Bobby Lewis (Daniel Quinn).

Powers arrives just in time to see Vaughn murder one of the
St. Mark's robbers in cold blood.

Vaughn takes careful aim with his 50 calibre Desert Eagle.

Vaughn lures the robber into picking up his gun so he can shoot him.

*Powers is too late to stop his partner from shooting an
unarmed robber.*

Kelly Daniels (Chelsea Field) working late into the night at home as she tries to figure out who the S.I.S. really are.

The final confrontation between Powers and Vaughn.

Lou Diamond Phillips and Scott Glenn take a moment off between shots to talk with the director, Mark Lester.

Eddie Brown, the first assistant cameraman (partially hidden) and Mark Irwin (Director of Photography) with the author Frank Sacks (writer/producer for Extreme Justice*).*

Behind-the-scenes on the last day of shooting. Lou Diamond Phillips, Frank Sacks, Chelsea Field, and Scott Glenn.

She tried to smile, but from the look on his face that wasn't going to cut it. As she cleared the hall and gazed directly at him, he raised a .357 magnum and, with both hands gripping the handle, turned it upside down so the trigger was in the air.

As the barrel went into his open mouth, she yelled out, "NO! DON'T!" But before she could say another word, Lloyd pulled the trigger. BLAM! The mesh screen behind his head was splattered with his blood.

Kelly screamed from the sound and the sight. She took one step toward him as a reaction to help. But it was over. "Oh, my God . . . Oh, no . . . no!" She had to look away, she was going to be sick. Kelly held her hand over her mouth and stumbled back to the phone in the kitchen to call the police.

In front of St. Peter's Bar, Angel sat on the sidewalk panhandling for change. He was dressed like a bum, but in the last hour and a half had actually picked up nearly seven bucks in loose change. Across the street, Powers and Vaughn had stayed in their position. Another fifty yards away, at the entrance to the alley, Larson sat in an unmarked car.

Driving toward them all was a late-model, open-topped Jeep. At the wheel was Bobby Lewis; next to him, Mark Franklin. In the back seat were two friends along for the show. They backed into an open space across the street from the bar.

Lewis and Franklin jumped out and the guys in back moved forward. Angel was the first to spot them, and raised his dirty shirt sleeve to alert the rest of the team. "Visitor team is on the field." Powers turned away from them as he was too close, walking a few steps with Vaughn before he spoke into his hidden mic: "End Zone, this is Quarterback. How's the view?"

Within the crowded bar, Cusack was sitting at the back, trying to be inconspicuous. It wasn't working. He was dressed like an overaged yuppie beach kid. He smiled at a pretty girl half his age as she passed by, then answered by talking into the Sony Walkman in his hand. He wore a headset and was wired into the squad. "Ready when you are," Cusack said.

Lewis and Franklin strolled across the avenue and walked right by Angel as they went into the bar. They stepped inside for only a moment to case it, and then came out. As they walked back to the Jeep, Franklin felt his partner was uneasy. He asked him, "What do you wanna do?"

Lewis answered, "I don't like it. San Diego's cooler. Cops around here can really fuck you up. Maybe we should book outta here?"

Franklin was a lot more sure about it. "Hey, Bobby, stop sweatin'. The cops won't bother us. . . . We're white."

Lewis still wasn't sure. "I don't know, bro', we know all the bars in 'S.D.' Up here, everything's a big question mark."

Franklin calmed him down. "You collecting pussy points today? It's a yuppie beach bar, dude! It's not like we're crashing an Army base or something!"

Lewis laughed in spite of himself, then reached into a large duffel bag in the back of the Jeep and took out a mean-looking pistol. Lewis had obviously changed his mind, and said so: "Okay . . . let's get rich!" He slapped the back of Franklin and told the two accomplices, "You guys sit tight and keep the wheels greased."

Lewis and Franklin walked back across the beach street dodging slow-moving traffic and looking very casual. They passed Angel one more time as they entered the crowded bar.

Inside, a mix of young singles were full of conversation and hormones. In a practiced series of moves, Lewis and Franklin drew their guns and K.O.'d the crowd. Accountants and secretaries recoiled in horror as the two perps took over center stage. Lewis had a smile on his face as he waved the big pistol above his head so those in the back could have a good look.

"Good afternoon, crime victims!" he called out. "Welcome to the Mark and Bobby show! You're about to get robbed by the best-lookin' thieves on the street!"

Cusack couldn't believe what he was hearing, this was "Amateur Time in Dixie."

The bar quieted quickly as the two would-be robbers pointed their weapons at the patrons. Cusack crouched down so he could speak into the radio, but kept his voice low. "It's going down. Right now!"

Just outside the door, Angel had to press his earpiece close-in so he could hear Cusack's words. He backed away from the door and pulled a small two-wheeled shopping cart loaded with junk along with him. He turned his head to check on the position of the two accomplices still sitting in the Jeep. Both of them were sunning themselves.

Farther down but on the same side of the street, Powers and Vaughn were getting ready to move into position. Powers passed the word, "The ball is in play."

Powers watched as Angel kept his back to him and used his body to shield his movement from the guys in the Jeep. He pulled a sawed-off shotgun from among the rubbish in the cart. He pumped a round into the chamber and nervously looked back at the two behind him.

Powers pressed his hand to his earpiece, trying to listen in through Cusack's mic on the inside. Powers was talking to no one in particular when he said, "Come on out, boys. . . . Don't fuck anybody up, just come on out and play with us."

Lewis was having a blast picking up a gold Rolex off the bar counter. He hopped the bar and pulled the cash out of the register, stuffing it all in his jeans. Cusack inched forward and thought he could get the drop on both of them provided he could get his gun out quickly. Franklin was getting impatient, "Okay, let's go!" Lewis hopped over the bar again and moved toward Cusack. Something had caught Lewis' eye. He said, "But wait! There's more! You get the fabulous Ginsu knives, the steak knives, and the Apple Magician . . . and . . ." He turned on the yuppie stockbroker next to Cusack. "This guy's watch! Okay, pal, take it off!" The stockbroker handed it over quickly.

Lewis looked back at Cusack; something was going through the kid's mind. He shot a quick glance at Franklin. Cusack almost drew his gun. Franklin saw something that was much more interesting than Lewis had seen, and walked toward Cusack. Both guns were on the Detective now. Franklin smiled, "On second thought, fuck the watch," he told Lewis. "Let's take the babe!"

The girl with the yuppie stockbroker was ready to faint. She wore an expensive-looking diamond bracelet on her wrist. The only thing Franklin had to do was stare at it before she said, "Here, take it! Just leave me alone." He leaned over and kissed her hand. Cusack was going nuts. All he wanted was a chance. Franklin continued to play the part, "That's the nicest, most generous rejection I've ever had. Could I have your phone number?" The girl couldn't believe it. "NO!" she said. Franklin acted disappointed, then smiled as he stuffed the bracelet in his pocket. "Hey, you never know until you ask, right?"

Cusack was ready to move on this jerk. He took one step forward just as Franklin pressed his gun against his head. "Don't move too fast there chilly-willy. What'cha got there? A cool Walkman? Let me have it." Cusack took off the headset and handed it to him." Cusack tried to act scared when he said, "Here, take it, man. Just don't hurt me, okay?" Franklin thought that was funny. "Hey, old man, don't have a heart attack."

Both "surfers" backed out of the bar together, Lewis throwing out one more parting wisecrack: "Thanks for the capital gains, folks."

Lewis and Franklin stepped out of the bar, turned, and stared straight into the double barrels of Angel's shotgun. "Don't fucking move, or your dead." Angel meant every word.

Across the street the other two perps saw Angel pull the weapon. The one who had taken the driver's seat didn't hesitate to race away from their parked position and gun it straight for Angel. Angel heard the jeep coming up from behind, but couldn't turn away from Lewis and Franklin as they still had guns in their hands.

Cusack had struggled to push his way through the crowd to get to the front door and was halfway there when he saw the Jeep smash into Angel and knock him ten feet into a concrete pillar. Powers and Vaughn ran across the street, their guns drawn.

Powers yelled to the people around them, "Get out of the way! Police!"

The Jeep had turned up the street toward the alley while Lewis and Franklin took off on foot down a sidewalk full of hundreds of people walking in and out of the beach stalls. As the Jeep turned the corner, it went head-on into another car.

They collided so hard, the kid in the passenger seat flew out over the top of the windshield and landed on the Jeep's front hood. He rolled off it and hopped up on the step on the driver's side, grabbing onto the roll bar as his partner put the car in reverse and floored it.

Larson now pulled up behind them to block their way and the two cars crashed into each other. The kid threw the Jeep back into first and the vehicle nearly did a wheelie as he popped the clutch and the Jeep lurched forward.

Cusack was checking on Angel, who was out cold with a concussion and a broken arm. The driver in the Jeep drove it onto the sidewalk to escape. He was headed straight for the two Detectives. Cusack had to grab Angel by the collar and drag him unconscious into the front entrance of the bar. The Jeep roared by, narrowly missing both of them.

As it passed, the driver threw it into second and barreled down the rest of the sidewalk. People leaped out of the way to save their lives as he drove it right through a half-dozen wooden tables stacked high with beach merchandise. Shoes, swim suits, and a thousand pairs of sunglasses exploded into the air! The kid holding on to the roll bar tucked himself in close to the driver so that he wouldn't have his head knocked off as the stalls and stands rushed by, inches from his back.

Larson had his car running parallel to the Jeep, steering with his right hand and using his left to fire at the two perps.

Cusack stepped out from the bar and in a shooter's stance used both hands to hold steady. From a hundred or more feet back, he unloaded his entire clip into the Jeep. His shots blew out one tire--and the back of the driver's head. Blood shot onto the windshield and all over his buddy, who was still hanging on until he caught a round in the leg. His grip on the roll bar loosened just as the Jeep went out of control and rolled completely over toward Larson's car on his right.

The kid hanging onto the driver's side was catapulted over the top of the Jeep as it flipped. He went through fifteen feet of air before bouncing off the roof of Larson's car and onto the street. Larson slammed on the brakes and jumped out. He ran over to the kid, who laid facedown, totally knocked out. Larson rolled him over with his foot, holstered his gun, and cuffed the guy as if he had taken down a steer at a rodeo.

Lewis and Franklin meanwhile had run like crazy, zigzagging through the crowd with Powers and Vaughn about a hundred feet behind. There were far too many people between the four for a clear shot.

Powers yelled at the top of his lungs for people to move, "CLEAR! POLICE! GET OUT OF THE WAY!" But Lewis and Franklin were both younger, faster, and putting distance between themselves and the cops.

With the four of them running, bystanders were being pushed to the ground and knocked over. And then, finally, the chase moved off the Venice beach sidewalk and across a small, grassy area toward an unused and deserted concrete building.

Powers and Vaughn had run full out for more than three blocks and were breathing hard as they approached the abandoned structure. Lewis and Franklin were far ahead and had ducked around a corner to catch their breath. They felt safe and exuberant . . . for the moment.

Franklin began laughing with the maniacal glee of an adrenaline rush. "Fuckin' A! We blew 'em off! I fought the law, and I won, I fought the law . . ."

Lewis knew better, "Shut the fuck up. Let's book it!"

Franklin was anything but sharp, and said, "What's the rush? They're miles behind us!"

Lewis told him the way it really was. "They toasted Ed and Chris, man! They're fucking history! This is serious shit! They're after our asses, amigo!"

Franklin snapped back into a token reality. "Oh, man . . . this is too intense."

They took off again down an alley, putting as much distance between them and the bar as possible. But they looked back in time to see Vaughn and Powers gaining on them! And the cops poured it on when they spotted their quarry.

Lewis and Franklin came to a T-intersection. They stopped for a moment, terrified. "Split up!" commanded Lewis.

Franklin took off. "See you on the other side, bro'."

They ducked into different alleys and ran like hell. Lewis found himself in an area that had formerly been a public picnic ground but had been abandoned. The concrete tables and all the walls had been tagged by the local gangs, and there wasn't a square inch not covered with graffiti.

Powers and Vaughn stopped at the place where the perps had split up. "We're never gonna find 'em if we wait for backup," said Powers. Vaughn was breathing the heaviest, but would never give up. He motioned for Powers to go left and said, "Who said anything about waiting?" He took off one way and Powers the other.

Franklin made the wrong turn and ran into an old locker room and public urinal. The place was a nightmarish maze of neglect: broken windows, dirty walls, and garbage. He went from one part to another looking for an escape, but there was none. Running around a corner into the locker area, he crouched down low, waiting for the cop to come in after him.

Powers ran up to the entrance but then slowed down, taking one step at a time. He held his gun with both hands, ready to fire. Staying close to the wall, he inched his way toward a corner. Then he halted momentarily, not knowing what he faced on the other side. In a quick move, he turned the corner and Franklin came up underneath his gun, running his shoulder into Powers' body, pushing them both back into a wall of broken lockers.

This knocked the wind out of Powers, but he came up quickly with a knee to the kid's groin and followed it with a quick fist to his solar plexus and another roundhouse punch to his temple. The young man was no match for Powers, and dropped to his knees, letting his pistol fall to the ground. Powers lifted him up and flung him back against a wire grating.

He had him handcuffed to it in a few seconds, and then picked up the kid's gun. A look of shock crossed his face. He took hold of the kid by the collar and made him look him in the eye. Jeff was mad. "Jesus! A pellet gun! I could have killed you, you fucking moron!"

A hundred yards away, Lewis was trapped. He'd entered a long alleyway with only one entrance and exit, the way he had come in. He got to the end of it and was about to try to scale the wall, but he decided to simply give up. He had nothing to lose. Vaughn entered the same alley and yelled out, "Don't move, don't turn around!" Lewis held his gun high above his head and turned around anyway--with a big smile on his face. Vaughn wasn't smiling. "Drop the gun . . . !"

The kid let it go and it bounced between them, sounding like cheap plastic instead of cold steel. Vaughn recognized the sound. Lewis told him, "All right, dude, you win! Gave you a hell of a run, though, huh? Worked off a few donuts."

Lewis was being cocky and casual about the whole thing. Vaughn didn't think it funny, nor did he yet let his guard down. He moved closer. He asked the kid, "What are you laughing about, asshole?" Lewis responded, "I know something you don't know. You don't have shit on me."

Vaughn didn't want to listen to this crap. He said, "Try Robbery-Assault."

Lewis laughed, "You *fucked up*, man! You got the wrong guys. How do you kill someone with a pellet gun? It's a toy, dude! We just wanted the money; just havin' fun."

Vaughn couldn't believe his ears. He was more than pissed off at this little wise-mouthed punk. He told him, "You're going away, junior."

Lewis laughed again. "Maybe to summer camp, but that's it, pops. I'm seventeen."

Vaughn was furious. "What did you say?"

Lewis laughed in his face again. "Everybody says I look older. I'm a juvy, scrode! They'll give me a week of cleaning freeways, then I'll be back cleaning out cash registers."

Vaughn was stunned. He lowered his gun. "That's a toy gun? Let me see that thing."

As Lewis took a step forward and reached down to the ground to pick it up, Powers silently walked in behind Vaughn and watched as the kid straightened up with the toy gun in his hand. He saw it coming, and called out, "NO, DAN!" Vaughn pumped three slugs into Lewis' chest, sprawling the boy backwards. He was dead before he dropped.

Vaughn took a long look at the body, holstered his gun, and turned to face Powers. "Self-defense, Jeff. You saw the whole thing."

Powers was too stunned to speak. Vaughn walked over to the body and leaned down to look closely at the gun. He acted surprised. "Shit, it's a pellet gun. How was I supposed to know? The kid was so stupid he drew down on me. Probably stoned. You saw the whole thing, right, Jeff?"

Powers gave him a long, cold look. Vaughn didn't like it. He asked him again, "Right, Jeff?" The tone in Powers voice betrayed his words: "Yeah, the whole thing." He didn't wait for Vaughn to say anything else, and started to walk away. Vaughn followed him down the alley and grabbed him by the shoulder from behind. Vaughn was nervous. "Don't get weird on me, Jeff."

Powers' anger raged inside, the ache he had felt was now pure pain. "Just stay away from me, Vaughn."

Dan recognized it for what it was: a threat. He let go of Powers' shoulder. "You really want to take me on over this piece of shit? He was trash, Jeff! That sick little fuck would've been out in three weeks if we'd let him go."

Powers did everything he could not to punch Vaughn in the face. His anger boiled over. "Let him go?! You never had any fucking intention of letting him go. You never let *anybody* go!" Powers had to get away. He turned and started walking.

Vaughn pulled his gun, and aimed it at Powers' back. He yelled out to him, "It's my word against yours, kid. And your rep ain't worth shit! Don't fuck with me, Jeff! Do you hear me!"

Jeff kept on walking and Vaughn slowly lowered his gun, watching his partner disappear around the corner. Vaughn turned back to look at the dead "surfer" still holding the pellet gun by the barrel.

Powers knew what he had to do next, and went straight to Police Headquarters to talk with Captain Shafer about what he'd just witnessed. Shafer was upstairs with the "suits" in a meeting. Powers paced the floor near his office until he caught the Captain on his way to another meeting down the hall.

"What can I do for you, Powers?"

Powers didn't have the time to make small talk. "Captain, what would you say if a member of the unit had a real problem with his partner. That is, if he felt his partner had killed a perp in cold blood?"

Powers had definitely caught the attention of the Captain. Shafer stopped walking and turned to confront him. "Just exactly what are you trying to tell me, Powers? Because right now my answer is, we'd take it up within the section."

Powers saw he was running into big trouble. "But, Captain, I saw Vaughn shoot the suspect. He wasn't even armed."

Shafer's blood pressure went right to the top. "First, don't ever talk like that to anybody about the S.I.S. Second, if it's Vaughn, then I'm certain you've got your story screwed up. And third, I don't need that kind of crap. I've spent a long time developing this unit and I don't need to be having some kinda bullshit tearing it down."

Powers had struck a nerve. "But Captain—"

Shafer interrupted, he wasn't going to listen to this anymore. "If you got a problem with Vaughn, get it straightened out with your partner. Understand, Powers?"

Shafer turned and walked away, not waiting for an answer. He left Powers with nothing but that same aching feeling in his stomach.

Powers went down to the briefing room and sat at a desk to type out his report of what had gone down. Other members of the squad were doing the same thing, although theirs certainly weren't going to read like his. Since Powers had been in the room, Vaughn had not bothered to look up or acknowledge his presence, though they sat just a few feet away from each other.

It was obvious to Larson that these two had been at it again. Larson was leaving, and tried to get them to lighten up. As he passed between them, he smiled and said, "Lovers' quarrel, boys?" He laughed at his own sense of humor and kept on walking.

The two were by themselves now, and Powers felt it was time to start pushing some of Vaughn's buttons. He went right for the throat. "How long you been gettin' away with murder . . . boss?"

Vaughn didn't react at all for a moment, then stood up and walked over to Powers' desk. He leaned in so close that only inches separated the two men, and, with a deadly glare he looked Powers in the eye and told him: "You say something like that outside this room and I'll bury you, kid." Then Vaughn pulled back, picked up his coat, and walked slowly toward the door. As he opened it, he turned back to Powers. "If I were you, I'd be worried about your future, not mine," Vaughn said.

Over the following few days and nights, Powers
thought about his next move and, for that matter,
whether he even had one. To go up against Vaughn
alone was a battle he knew could not be won. Turning
on Vaughn was not merely a case of one against one,
it was something you just didn't do. Cops lived in
their own world--period. And, though there was a
library full of books about all the laws they had to
live by and enforce, the most important ones for the
men in blue had always been the unwritten rules, the
ones that were *never* to be broken. Jeff knew that at
the top of the list was a belief that their special line of
work demanded an allegiance to each other first . . .
and then the public. There was a silent pact wherein
they judged their own kind first and never just fed
their brothers to the press. It was very simple: You
never turned another cop in to the public first, no
matter what the offense, because cops had their own
way of taking care of those who broke the law within
their ranks. They disciplined their own because no
one on the outside understood the kinds of pressures
they all had to endure. There was a ring of truth to
the rule in which they believed, and it was a rule that,
almost to the man, each of them had agreed to
respect--once they were part of the team. It was a rule
that throughout history had made perfect sense and
at other times had ultimately been responsible for the
downfall of entire civilizations. It was a rule that
most cops had kept and that, if violated, usually

destroyed the accuser as well as the accused.
For Powers, this last confrontation with Dan
Vaughn had turned his internal pain into a mind-
numbing level of guilt. He couldn't live with it
and yet he might not live at all if he pushed it any
further.

His whole life had "turned south" in a big way. He
could no longer function. For the past ten days since
he'd moved away from Kelly, he had been living in a
motel room and, today, going to Lloyd's funeral was
the first time he had done anything since Vaughn had
murdered the kid a week before. In the interim, Powers
had taken a couple of days off to get a handle on his
own psyche. So far, he was doing a piss-poor job and
he felt terrible.

As he drove toward the cemetery to Mike Lloyd's
funeral he tried to unscramble the events that had
overtaken him since he'd joined the S.I.S. Not a lot
made sense anymore, including his ability to continue
working with the unit.

He parked his car and silently joined the other men
of the Special Investigation Section as they gathered
around Lloyd's coffin. It was late in the day, and the
soft light filtering through the trees gave the graveyard
a calm, serene feeling. A small wind blew through the
leaves as the S.I.S. stood together to honor one of its
own.

The minister was finishing the last rites, but Powers' own thoughts were drifting in and out of what was
being said. At one point, Vaughn expressed the feelings for most of the men when he said, "And when he
died, Mike Lloyd was still an officer in the Department,

and a member of this team. He will always be a member of this team."

A few distant relatives and neighbors who knew Lloyd sat in one short row and cried as the coffin was slowly lowered into the ground. Powers watched the top of it disappear and then looked up as the group began to break away.

Standing in the distance, partially hidden in the shade was Kelly. Jeff knew he'd caught her eye, but she abruptly turned and started walking quickly to her car. He hurried to catch up with her, taking hold of her arm as she opened the car door. "Are you okay?" he asked.

She wasn't there to talk to, and kept it short. "Yeah." Powers stumbled, "So, did he, uh, talk before . . ."

Kelly was angry and hurt. "No."

She started to get in her car again, and then changed her mind. There was one last thing she had to say, and it came from deep within. "How many people have to die before someone comes clean?" He said nothing. She asked him point-blank, "Will *you* go on record?" Powers felt trapped. "No . . . I'm handling this my way."

Kelly knew better. She knew that everything they had ever meant to each other, everything that both aspired to be was on the line. Tears filled her eyes as she told him, "You want to protect the Department, but you don't mind if they turn L.A. into Beirut? You don't mind when they become judge, jury, and executioner? Maybe I missed something . . . but when, exactly, did we abolish the Constitution of the United States, just so we could protect the fucking Department?! They are not going to protect *you*, Jeff."

That was it. She had nothing left to say, and he felt there was nothing left for him at all. He watched as her car pulled away, leaving him standing all alone, again.

Lieutenant Devlin was busy pushing paper across her desk. One thing she had learned about Internal Affairs: If it didn't bury you with cases to investigate, it certainly buried you in paperwork. She was not happy, and when Powers unexpectedly entered her office she knew the day had really turned to shit. With a sardonic look on her face, she welcomed him in typical Devlin fashion: "Decide to turn yourself in for the greater good, Powers?"

He pulled up a chair without being asked. She raised an eyebrow signaling he'd better be careful.

"I need your help," he said.

"I wouldn't piss in your mouth if your teeth were on fire," she told him. It was a typical Devlin remark.

"What if I gave you a case? A capital case. A Detective gunning down an unarmed perp in cold blood." He waited for a response.

She sat forward, interested, and had one key question: "Witnesses?"

He hesitated, then looked up. "Right in front of you."

Devlin reached for a sheaf of paper and laid out forms in front of him. "Okay, you got my attention. Who's the shooter?"

Powers crossed the line and told her: "Vaughn, my partner."

Her look of disappointment caught him by surprise. She sat back in her chair and her shoulders dropped. From the expression on her face, you could tell the interest was gone. She said, "S.I.S. I should've known that's where you'd end up. You can fill out the forms, but I can't promise you anything."

Powers had never liked her, but especially hated what she'd just told him. "What do you mean? I'm talking about murder!" Devlin thought he knew the game and was surprised by his naiveté. "Do you know how many 'Officer Involved' shootings there are in a year? Only a few are ever recommended for prosecution. It's an uphill battle."

Powers was incensed. "A minute ago, you were loaded for bear." She went on, "Internal Affairs specializes in corruption: cops taking payoffs and running scams. Shootings aren't our bread and butter."

Powers was on tilt. If she shut him down, there was nowhere to go. He told her, "You're afraid of the S.I.S. You're fucking chickenshit!"

Devlin couldn't meet his eyes. She was defensive, her tone was no longer one of intimidation. "I'm just doing my job."

He let her know exactly what he thought. "Your job? You're not doing your job! You're covering your ass! You're so fucking righteous when you're trying to bury *me* six feet under, but bring on someone with juice, like Vaughn, and suddenly you're thinking about your pension!"

He got up from his seat, nearly knocking it over. He wasn't through with her yet. His jaw tightened. "You're pathetic. You'll even offer the paperwork, so nobody can say you turned me away. Fuck you!" He moved to the door, and let it all out: "Fuck you, lady, because now, now I am dead."

He slammed the door behind as he left. If he'd looked back at her face, and into her eyes, he would have known that his words had struck home.

In another time and another place, Jeff Powers would have had a simple life: a family, a regular job. All of those things crossed his mind as he sat with Kelly in front of her tape recorder in the living room. There had been no place else to go, and by attrition he now sat opposite her, about to say things that he would have never imagined possible.

The pain that had built up inside him had not simply subsided, it had left him paralyzed. And though what he was about to say would release a lot of pressure, the truth was that there was no moral victory, no exultation from cleansing his soul, no feeling better. There was just a sense of personal honor he had to follow. He had realized that Kelly was right. It was wrong to be the judge, jury, and executioner—even in the world *he* lived in.

For Kelly, it was different, although it was anything but a celebration. This was the kind of story that put your name on the reporter's map, on the front page. But Page One had ceased being the goal; it was much much more than that now. It was a cleansing of all the things that had split them apart. Things that taken away their respect for each other and had begun to destroy the love between them. Only now, as they sat together for the first time in weeks, did there seem to be a light of hope for their future.

Kelly also knew she was doing this for reasons that went beyond their personal lives. Things that had struck a different chord within her. And though she was a little selfish by nature, and this feeling inside her was new, it was a feeling that rang true to who she wanted to be. However, the process of getting there had nearly killed him and almost destroyed their love for each other.

This had been more than just difficult, and she felt that the circumstances that had led them to this point ultimately controlled them completely. Each of them now felt calm for the first time as they faced the truth together.

Jeff picked up the tape recorder and turned it on. He spoke evenly, slowly. He carefully chose his words. "I was recruited into the Special Investigation Section by Dan Vaughn, my former partner. I want to make it clear that not every S.I.S. cop is a bad cop. And that this unit didn't start out bad. We were supposed to be an elite section. We were supposed to take the worst of the worst off the streets. . . . Somewhere along the line, that changed."

Dan Vaughn was asleep on the couch when the telephone started to ring. At first, he thought it was part of his dream, but then realized that didn't make sense since in it he was somewhere on a beach with Sheila. When he finally opened his eyes, he was surprised to see the TV still on—as it had been all night.

It was difficult to sit upright, because he was stiff and had basically drunk himself to sleep in the den. He thought, to himself, that whoever was on the other end was pretty damn insistent, as it must have rung ten times before he finally picked up the receiver. It took only one word for Dan to recognize Captain Shafer's voice.

Shafer, as usual, didn't bother with any light chatter. "Dan, hey, Vaughn, is that you? Have you seen the papers? The TV? Shit, Dan, we've been blown sky high. Powers has fucked us six ways to Sunday. Dan? . . . VAUGHN?"

Dan never bothered to say a word. He just hung up. He slowly stood up and walked to the front door. He found the newspaper just outside. When he came back in, he tuned in the television to a local news program and unwrapped the morning edition. He couldn't believe his eyes. The headline of the paper was a living nightmare. "SECRET S.I.S. UNIT EXPOSED. L.A.P.D. UNDER FIRE." Vaughn was so thrown by what he was reading, he didn't hear Powers' Jeep pull up in front of the house.

Outside, Kelly sat next to Jeff and felt more than just concerned about what he was going to do next. She said to him, "You know, you could just as well have sent your badge to him. You don't have to do this."

She was wrong. He was not without fear, but it wasn't going to stop him. "I can't avoid Vaughn for the rest of my life. I want him to hear it from me. Don't worry, I'll be right back."

Vaughn had finished reading all he needed to, and sat transfixed, watching the TV screen. He clutched the newspaper as if he were trying to throttle it. On the tube, another city official was taking the heat: "S.I.S.? I never heard of them. Hard to believe they were part of our distinguished Police Department. This information is hard to grasp. I'm sure someone was in charge, but we need time to look into it."

Next up was Captain Shafer. "Of course we have a Special Investigations Section. I don't deny that. But this is the same old story. You, the press, don't give a damn about what we face. You'd just as soon protect the violent criminals and let our men go to hell! Well, we've learned how to treat repeat offenders, and I just wish you'd learn how to have some integrity in what you report!" The Captain was defensive as he went on: "Gentlemen, there is a real crooked slant in the media. Our *heroes* get an inch in the paper and *this biased trash* gets three pages. You call that fair? You don't know what fair is!"

Shafer had been caught by the press coming out a side door of Police Headquarters and was obviously embarrassed, since the press hounded him all the way to his car. "No comment," he finally repeated, over and over again. Vaughn just stared in disbelief. He didn't hear the knock at the door.

Powers let himself in. Vaughn stood up and there he was. In a calm but very dangerous tone Vaughn said, "Who the fuck do you think you are, Powers?"

Jeff told him, "It's over, Vaughn."

Vaughn's hate for what Powers had done to the unit couldn't be held in check. "Over? It hasn't even started, you cocksucker! You think you can fuck with me and then just turn your back!?"

Powers didn't give an inch: "You think *I* fucked you over! What a joke! You feel righteous? Wait until

I.A. and the City Council hears what you really do."

Vaughn raised his eyebrows. For Vaughn this was more than anything he could have ever imagined.

Powers was not unafraid of Vaughn. He went on: "Yeah, I'm going to tell them, all right. The papers are just a start. I'm gonna tell everyone who'll listen. Because *you* aren't the L.A.P.D., Vaughn, *I* am. You're just the field officer of a unit you've turned into a motherfucking death squad!"

Vaughn boiled with rage. He let out a scream of pure hate as he lunged at Powers, slamming them both into the wall. They fought like angry dogs, pounding, growling, ripping, and biting. They wouldn't let go of each other and smashed into tables and chairs. Their heads butted against each other, their fists became bloodied as they careened off the walls, pushing and pulling.

They threw each other into the television, sending it and them exploding onto the floor, where they rolled until Powers had the chance to use his legs. He kicked Vaughn off, sending him reeling through the French glass door to the kitchen. The man's impact splintered it like balsa wood into a hundred pieces.

Powers stood up and ran in to finish him, but Vaughn raised his boot and caught him in the groin. Vaughn quickly got up off the kitchen floor and landed two hard punches in Jeff's midsection, knocking the wind out of the younger man and doubling him over. But Powers grabbed hold of Vaughn's shirt and with all his might sent him headfirst into a wall of shelving that crashed to the floor.

Kelly had heard the commotion, and now came

running into the house. She moved into the kitchen and directly into a tremendous backhand as Vaughn caught her across the mouth and sent her flying into a wall, knocking her unconscious.

Vaughn turned back to Powers and began to choke him. He was so crazed and pumped with hate that he lifted Powers off his feet and threw him onto the countertop. He never let go as he leaned over him and with all his might tried to choke the last breath from Powers' body. Jeff was blacking out. He could only use his thumbs, pushing them into Vaughn's eyes to force him back. Vaughn screamed out in pain, nearly blinded.

Powers slid off the countertop and stumbled as both tried to regain their senses. Again they grabbed each other, each trying to fling the other off his feet.

They turned in a circle and like a centrifuge went careening out the huge bay window of the kitchen. The collision sent shards of glass everywhere. The two men landed with a hard thud on the ground in the front yard. A thousand pieces of glass covered their bodies and had cut their faces and arms.

Vaughn was the first to get to his feet, and he kicked at Powers' face as the man tried to rise on one knee. The blow sent Powers into a backward somersault but he rolled with it and stood up on both legs.

Vaughn took two steps forward and caught him with a roundhouse punch to the jaw, and then another to the gut, and a third to the side of the head. The blows propelled Powers back, and he staggered as everything around him swirled. Vaughn charged him again and drove both of them through a wooden gate.

Vaughn was the first to get up, and now he grabbed

a broken two by four on the ground. He raised it over his head and came down as hard as he could, hoping to crush Powers' skull, but Jeff rolled away from the blow at the last second.

Jeff struggled to his feet. They circled each other and then Vaughn swung the two by four wildly left to right and then back again. Powers barely avoided both swings, but caught the third one in the ribs, which cracked from the hit. He buckled over from the pain but held on to the wood with one arm over it, until Vaughn yanked it from his grasp and swung it again. But Jeff took hold of it this time and came up with a leg to Vaughn's groin, forcing him to let go. Powers used the same two by four as a battering ram and sent the end straight into Vaughn's stomach.

The hit dropped Vaughn to his knees. He looked up, unable to stand, as Powers threw the wooden plank to the ground and smashed his fist straight into Vaughn's nose, shattering it completely. Then he took hold of Vaughn's collar with one hand, and in a series of incredible punches smashed into his face again and again until Vaughn's entire face was bloodied, black-and-blue. When Powers finally let go, Vaughn fell back to the ground totally spent.

Powers had all the advantage now but was out of control. He slowly walked around behind Vaughn, placed his arm around his neck, and began to strangle him to death.

Kelly, meanwhile, had awakened and now stumbled out a side door and ran to the two figures. As Powers tried to squeeze the life out of Vaughn with all the strength he had left, his victim gasped for air and, with one hand, reached down to his ankle to get hold of his other gun. His fingers took hold of the small revolver. Vaughn was about to pass out but pulled it from the holster.

Kelly saw, and screamed, "Jeff, he's got a gun!"

Vaughn raised it, blindly firing a shot toward Powers' face, but Jeff moved his head to the side and a bullet went right by his ear. With one arm still around Vaughn's neck, Powers took hold of the gun with his free hand. Vaughn had nearly lost consciousness. Suddenly, Powers released his choke hold, stood up, and in one motion aimed the gun at Vaughn.

Vaughn opened his eyes and rose up on his elbows, his face covered in bloodied dirt, his nose pushed an inch from where it had been before. He'd lost the fight but now he challenged Powers once again. "Go ahead, do it! Come on, Powers!"

Jeff looked down the gunsight at Vaughn. His finger tightened on the trigger. Vaughn stared at him, ready to die like a zealot. But Powers lowered the gun and eased the hammer down. He took a step backward, but still held the gun on Vaughn. And then, Powers reached for his belt and tossed his badge so that it landed on Vaughn's chest.

Powers told him, "If I shot you, I'd be just like you . . . and I'm not. I'm through, all right, I quit."

Powers backed up another few steps. He opened the cylinder on the .38 and emptied all the bullets in his hand and tossed them away. He threw the empty gun down.

He turned to Kelly and she came to his side. They had to support each other as they walked back toward the car.

Vaughn was stunned. He could not believe Powers had let him live. But he was still bitter and as full of hate as he'd ever been. He yelled out to them as he got to his feet, "You tell your girlfriend it doesn't mean dick! Nobody gives a fuck about what the papers say!"

Kelly and Jeff climbed in the Jeep. Vaughn staggered after them, yelling as loud as he could to be sure they heard what he said: "YOU CAN'T HURT ME, POWERS ... YOU HEAR ME!! IT DOESN'T MEAN DICK! PEOPLE WANT THE S.I.S., THEY WANT US TO DO WHAT WE'RE DOING."

Powers turned on the ignition and they began slowly to pull away. Kelly glanced over at Jeff. "Are you okay?" she asked, soothingly.

He was bleeding, he was bruised, but for the first time the real pain he'd felt inside had gone away, and he told her. "I'm ... okay." Powers smiled at her and stepped on the accelerator. Behind them, Vaughn stumbled into the street. He staggered down the middle of it watching them pull out of his driveway. And with all that he had within himself, he opened his arms wide and looked to the sky above, screaming at the heavens, "YOU HEAR WHAT I'M SAYING? NOBODY CARES! DEEP DOWN, THEY LOVE WHAT WE DO! THEY ALL FUCKING LOVE IT!!! YOU HEAR ME ... THEY ALL FUCKING LOVE IT!"

- EPILOGUE -

Detective Dan Vaughn was killed six months later during an S.I.S. shootout by an armed felon.

Detective Jeff Powers is working undercover for an Internal Affairs Division in Michigan.

The S.I.S. continues to operate in Los Angeles. It remains the only permanent unit of its kind in the United States.

Part III

BEHIND THE SCENES

The behind-the-scenes incidents that occurred during the making of the film *Extreme Justice*, and ultimately shaped it, are a story unto themselves. They influenced this book in ways that, I feel, require a detailed review. Simply said, I believed that making the movie was going to be my epitaph. . . .

Extreme Justice did not start out, money-wise, like anything near what it wound up. In its infancy, it was a $250,000 low-budget exploitation picture, destined to go straight to video. In the end, it turned out to be a multi-million-dollar production with a worldwide distribution assured.

In between were four years of continual ups and downs, and finally a story of the tail wagging the dog, that encompassed: four directors, five false production starts, thirty-nine screenplay rewrites, forty-seven budgets, a series of stars who were in, then out, and then in again, mercurial egos, hundred of thousands in financial discrepancies, spies watching spies, suspected wiretaps, an FBI investigation . . . and enough intrigue and secrecy on the set to easily compete with the suspense taking place in front of the cameras.

And, for those who might say this list isn't long enough to qualify for the "Most Troubled Production Oscar," then let's throw in one stabbing, two lawsuits, three shootings, four firings, the threat of a teamster strike, a Director's Guild shutdown, a Screen Actor's Guild boycott, two injured stunt men, and one near-riot during the course of production.

Nevertheless, in the end, my own reflections place *Extreme Justice* as a once-in-a-lifetime event. That the film was made at all is a testament to talent, good luck, and prayer.

IN THE BEGINNING

For years, everyone following the machinations of the film biz has been reading about problems that surface when you first try to get a movie made. A number of people associated with this film will affirm, however, that the course of events that preceded production of *Extreme Justice* compared admirably with the most trying experiences of their lives.

As for myself, making the movie reminded me of a nameless Hollywood Producer who showed up one day in our film class at San Francisco State, circa 1969. He filled our eager young minds with words that haunted me during the making of *Extreme Justice*. To quote the miserable sonofabitch: "None of you are going to make it in the movie business! You will waste your lives trying to break into a closed system. Be smart, don't waste your youth, your energy, and your optimism. Change the direction of your lives before its too late! Get out! Get out NOW, while you still can!"

Was he right? It doesn't matter. Making movies should be classified as a chronic disease. Once bitten, you're a lifer. And I'm sure it didn't stop the other true believers. Thank God, it didn't stop me. But for those of you contemplating entering this world as a profession, the following may give you some insight into what you are about to embrace. As for the rest of you—who are *un*interested—be thankful you found something else to do.

ACT I

To begin the tale, it makes sense to put a little perspective on what it takes these days to raise millions of dollars to finance a motion picture.

Overall, there are about 415 feature-length films made each year. This number includes both domestic as well as international productions, both studio and independently made pictures (around 160/255 films, respectively). And, while collectively these pictures gross $5 billion dollars in cinema tickets sold, the average studio picture is made for around $22 million, whereas the average independently made film costs only $3 million or so. Adding in the costs for prints and advertising--another $10 million for big pictures--and you start to get a feel for why the emphasis in the movie business is on the last word: "business."

Let there be no doubt about it, in today's film-world financial climate the word "business" is preeminent and, unfortunately, dictates far too many important creative decisions surrounding the making and distribution of motion pictures worldwide.The irony is that some films can still manage to survive and end up being creative extensions of man's best artistic nature. As we all know, a great film often incorporates *all the arts within a single medium*.However, when you start talking in the millions, financial and creative considerations become an immovable object colliding with an unstoppable one. When they collide on a daily basis, you've got yourself a succession of headaches that are grist for a hundred TV commercials.

That the above is common knowledge among those inside and outside the industry does not help when you enter the battle. The fact is, in Hollywood it is nearly impossible to get sympathy for your problems because problems are simply considered a *de rigueur* part of the business.

STAINLESS STEEL

From the day I left film school, I wanted to be a producer. However, I was quickly forced into writing instead. Without big bucks to buy a bestseller or without having an established directorial name that will attract top literary material from the agents, you aren't left with much in hand--and beginners don't make movies without a screenplay. At the same time, *writing* is the most cost-effective and fastest way to get yourself going.

Even if you haven't got a completed screenplay, you may come up with an idea so strong it can carry you a long way toward getting a picture made. That is precisely what happened in October 1988 on the day I read the first *Los Angeles Times* story about the S.I.S., the Special Investigations Section of its police department.

The first few paragraphs of that article established the premise of a secret group of detectives watching crime happen in order to nail someone on what can be a tougher charge. Not much more needed be said for me to get my own creative wheels moving. At the time, I was looking for an idea that could be made into a low-budget ($250,000) exploitation film that, I assumed, would go straight to video and never be seen in a theater. Having just produced my first film for $175,000, this would be at least a small step up.

From a producer's point of view, *Stainless Steel* (the picture's first name) fit all the necessary criteria: It could be shot locally, you didn't need to build sets, you didn't need stars or skilled union craftsman or even special effects. It was an idea you could express in twenty-five words or less to an investor, and it fit perfectly into the action genre--which meant it could have potential international interest.

Within two months, I had a script in hand but had been unable to raise ten cents after asking a number of different sources. No one I met had enough interest to put up the money. They either said it was because the film wouldn't have any stars (how could it? for this estimated price, people spent more money remodeling their Beverly Hills kitchens) or that it was too low-budget and/or I didn't have a name director attached. Not having a wealthy relative who was willing to give me a quarter-million dollars, I was apparently finished before I'd gotten started. The fact was, all the reasons I felt made it a good project were in turn used against it as reasons for *not* getting it funded. So much for logic!

However, experience from producing a previous film told me it was obviously time to shift gears: I upped the budget, unhooked myself from the low-budget director I couldn't sell, and figured out how to get a "name" on board without paying out any money. I used a standard movie ploy: Offer somebody something no one else will; that is, I'd see if I could rope in a star by holding out the possibility of letting him or her also direct his/her first feature film.

To stimulate some possibilities, I opened the voluminous player's directory, which has photos of thousands of actors. When I had reached the "J's," I thought I'd found the perfect star/director. I called the star's manager, made the pitch, flew to his then-current loca-

tion in Arizona, met for three hours, and we had a deal
... of sorts.

Here I was with a known commodity who had
starred in several successful TV series, never made it in
films, but nonetheless would fill a starring role nicely,
and had directed several bits for television. He agreed
he would let me use his name as part of the package
without my putting up any money. His manager negotiated the deal, I drafted a one-page letter for us to sign
with bailout clauses for all, and then went around to try
to build a cast and crew around him.

My next stop was the February 1989 American Film
Market, the AFM.

Somebody once called the AFM enclave "the K-
Mart of the film world." Perhaps at one time this was a
fair analysis, as it looked at one time more like a bazaar.
But that is certainly not the case today. For those not
familiar with it, it was established in 1981 by a handful
of independent international filmmakers/distributors
as a place for buyers and sellers to present their ideas,
their films, and create an effective international and
independent film market. Skeptics were everywhere
the first few years, and then suddenly the AFM had
matured into one of the three most important international film markets in the world. (The other two were
Cannes in the South of France every May, and MIFED,
which takes place in Milan, Italy, in the autumn.)

Today, the AFM is an established and respected
organization representing more than a hundred companies that make up the most successful independent
production and distribution companies in the business. Add in those peripheral indy's (independents),

who pay for a week's participation and take a hotel room during the AFM convention, plus several thousand buyers who fly in from around the world, and you end up with a unique once-a-year event now set at Loew's Santa Monica Hotel on the beach.

If you can get past the elaborate AFM security setup, you have access under one roof to some of the best and worst people in the business. (The trick is knowing how to tell them apart). From *Zomboids Invade Earth* to *The Terminator*. From guys who have more cash to spend than you can believe to people walking the halls trying to pick your pocket and your brain. It is truly an eclectic mix of film mavens.

With *Stainless Steel* under my arm, I walked in and out of fifty different suites that week, seeking interest in my new $6 million-dollar quasi-star package. I wound up trying to do business with a European-based distributor who promised to help me and said he could attract his foreign clientele into putting up pre-sale contracts in exchange for foreign rights, as a way to get all the production funds raised.

I spent the next couple of months preparing to meet him in Cannes. I put together brochures, sent him encouraging faxes, called him several times a month to try to keep him excited, and built what I felt was an Oscar-winning team around the lead star/director. I also added in other key creative elements and cashed in my Pan Am mileage for a free round-trip seat to the South of France for the May 1989 Cannes Film Festival.

For those unfamiliar with Cannes, I won't attempt to encapsulate in writing this strange but wonderful event other than to say that nothing I have ever read has truly captured this enchanting, addictive, and totally crazy week in southeastern France on the Côte d'Azur. It is an experience that must be made firsthand to appreciate.

(What Cannes and the AFM shared in common for my film was the general reaction the story elicited from the foreign buyers. Well before the movie became a reality, the international buyers I met at the AFM in Santa Monica and then in Cannes during the '89 Film Festival showed early signs of real interest in the subject matter.)

After I'd pitched the story in only twenty-five words or less, a foreign film distributor inevitably looked shocked and dismayed (if he or she hadn't dozed off), after hearing about the existence of the S.I.S. In their words, they said the S.I.S. was a "fascist" organization. And though it is a term that Americans relate to history, it is a word Europeans use in their everyday vocabulary.

These same independent film buyers wondered out loud how the S.I.S. could even exist within our law enforcement system. Another reaction this wily group shared in common was its underlying glee in discovering something new—negative, that is—to say about the U.S.A. It was as if they had just discovered that *their* country was not the only one with a police force that had the potential to get seriously out of control.

Once I saw their positive reactions, I spent the next ten days pitching to every foreign buyer who would listen. I stopped people on the beach, in the restaurants, at the theaters, in their hotel rooms, their yachts, their villas, and, after midnight, in the discos. In the end, I had spent thousands of dollars to promote *Stainless Steel*, while the foreign distributor I had earlier courted failed to do anything. I needed to make a new movie, not new friends. From a pure financial perspective, I was still nowhere.

However, I had aroused international interest. Nearly every foreign buyer I spoke to about the S.I.S. loved the idea. But I knew what the problem was: I didn't have the credibility to put it over the top.

I left Cannes buoyed by the reception to the script but without a dime of production financing in hand. I'd had a hundred meetings—but talk is anything but cheap on the French Riviera, now, when a single drink can run as high as $35 dollars. I told myself it had been a good experience ... and then remembered: Experience is what you get when you don't get what you want.

Once back in Los Angeles, I continued following up by fax, phone, and Fed Ex with those I'd encountered, and then one Sunday morning found myself reading the cover story to the entertainment calendar section of the *Los Angeles Times*. There, in all its ten-thousand-word glory was a fascinating in-depth piece on a new movie promoter who had just come to town. The feature stated right upfront, in black-and-white, that the guy on the front cover had $50 million cash to play the game with, and was going to be the next "Hollywood Mogul." He was, also, very independent, and was going to do it *his* way in Hollywood.

Along with quite a few other would-be producers in town, I was already calling this Japanese moneybags before I had left for Cannes but had not yet gotten past his secretary or assistants. I'd heard about him early on. Nothing in tinseltown travels as fast as rumors about fresh money. After reading the article, I continued to make calls to him now that I was back in L.A.--but still got no response. Then I changed mediums and followed up with a series of faxes. Finally, I got the script in the door and an appointment, only to discover I was one of 300 meetings he had been taking during that period as he looked for the right project.

In my first meeting with him, I must admit to having been very impressed: We sat in *his* office, in *his* building, on *his* block--which he had just bought, *for cash*. In our very first conversation he told me that the numbers cited by the newspaper were wrong, very wrong. He did not have $50 million, he had $200 million to make movies. CASH!

He seemed to appreciate my incessant pounding on his company door, and, miracle of miracles, out of the 300 meetings, I turned out to be the lucky one that was going to be his first deal!

But then it took three arduous months to negotiate a contract with his lawyer. This was followed by five more months in meetings and three major rewrites of the script. In the end, not a thing happened. It was an agonizing experience for both of us . . . though perhaps a little more so for him. (Later, I was told by two sources that he was getting so frustrated over his personal and business life at the time, that his blood pressure would cause him to literally pass out when he blew his top. If this were a contagious "producer's disease," then half of Hollywood today would be unconscious at any given moment.)

Further, although the city's most important newspaper had stated right there, for all to read, just how
much money this guy had and then he actually qua-
drupled the amount in a face-to-face conversation, this
particular Japanese money source dried up faster than
a drop of water in the desert. To date, he has had no
string of film hits, or string of film anything for that
matter. By the time he and I had parted company, he'd
spent $36K on *Stainless Steel* and I'd wasted about five
months of my time. It took two more excruciating
months merely to negotiate my way *out* of the deal.
During the period when I was entangled with this
mislabeled mogul, I had tried to keep my TV star/
director happy ... but uninformed of my impending
failure with the Japanese moneyman.

The same bad luck held true for the European-
based distributor, who continued to try and cling to the
project even though his efforts hadn't added a dime to
the kitty and we didn't have an agreed-upon contract.

As I'd already learned, you are dead in the movie
business unless you keep moving, so I called the star's
manager and told him it was over. He went ballistic
when I told him it wasn't going to work. He threatened, cussed, and sent me a nasty letter but, in the end,
realized for better or for worse that it wasn't to be.

Once again I found myself, one year later, at the
February 1990 American Film Market in Santa Monica,
starting anew. By now I had a dozen different versions
of the script—and of the budget. I again made the
rounds, looking for a new international sales group.

In addition, I continued to try to meet individual foreign distributors on my own. Again, another fifty meetings later, I had effectively made little concrete, cash-in-the-bank progress.

When the AFM was over, I decided to try contacting all the L.A.-based indy production companies that could finance the film. I also called on a number of the studios. Over the next six months, the rejection letters I received filled up a huge file in my cabinet.

Once more, I headed for Cannes, but this time went with a lawyer/friend who coincidentally wanted to go there for a vacation. Just before leaving Los Angeles, one of the indy companies in L.A. had begun to express interest in the script. Its head of development promised to wire me in with his boss, who owned the company, and now set up a meeting with him at the prestigious Carlton Hotel in Cannes.

By this time I was beginning to run into faces at Cannes that I had pitched the script to at either the two previous AFMs or the prior year's Cannes Festival. I got lots of encouragement but no money. I placed calls back to Los Angeles to try to firm up the meeting with the guy at the Carlton. The development exec told me I had to pick up the ball; he'd done everything he could to set it up.

The company, known as Kodiak Films, was run and owned by a Mr. Wolf Schmidt. (Kodiak's track record was mostly lower-budgeted pictures--with one exception, *The Fourth War*, which had proven to be a box-office disaster.) It took three attempts before I finally got by his appointment secretary, who stood in the hall and covered the doors to the rooms with great skill. Once allowed in, I was led into a plush three-room suite that overlooked all of Cannes and the Mediterranean from the most glamorous locale in town.

Mr. Schmidt was surrounded by assistants, his lawyer, and a couple of foreign buyers. His first comments were, "I don't have time for pitches, I'm here to sell. Not buy. You've got two minutes."

Fifteen minutes later, his last comments were, "If this story is true, then you've got a deal." I left him with several scripts, and had myself convinced this guy might actually make the movie.

Once back in L.A., it took another six weeks to negotiate a deal with his in-house lawyer. The film was to be a $1.5 million exploitation piece that, he said, we could start shooting in ninety days. During that time he continued to send the script out around the world to his foreign buyers to determine their level of interest.

The response he received was so positive that he then decided to up the budget and make a better-quality film. He also decided that we needed more script changes, and I started to do more rewriting. I also began working on a $3 million dollar budget. As the months rolled on, Mr. Schmidt began collecting more indications of interest from his worldwide contacts, but still the picture didn't get started. At last, after a series of additional rewrites, I was given the green light to go after a director.

The problem was to find a director who could make a picture on a short schedule of about three weeks and yet who could also deliver something you would want to watch when he had finished.

I interviewed several directors, and upon meeting

John Llewellyn Moxey, knew I'd found the one to do it. He had thirty years' experience. Though he was in his sixties, he still possessed the vision and energy that, when combined with his track record, told me he could deliver. John had directed dozens of movies for television and knew what it took to get a high degree of quality under severe time constraints. We worked on the script over another six-month period and I started looking for stars to fit in the three major roles.

I don't remember exactly how, but one day I ended up in the office of an agent's manager named Lloyd Bloom. In forty-five minutes he'd helped me put together a multi-million-dollar package using his clients for our three leads: Ken Wahl of *Wiseguy* fame, Robert Davi, and Kim Cattrall. Wahl was to play the lead of Detective Jeff Powers, Davi was to be Detective Dan Vaughn, and Ms. Cattrall would be the female reporter, Kelly.

The package looked great on paper, as Wahl had just been paid $1.75 million to play the lead in *The Taking of Beverly Hills*, a $25 million-dollar studio-distributed extravaganza. For $55,000 down, we could lock in, on paper, all three of them if Mr. Bloom also got to be Executive Producer: $25,000 to Wahl, $20,000 to Bloom, and $5,000 each to Davi and Cattrall. It was a package deal for all his clients; it was like one-stop shopping. Lloyd Bloom felt the picture and package would do really well, and so did we.

That took us into the fall of 1990. With a few more rewrites, we upped the budget another half-million or so. Mr. Schmidt starting closing more deals around the world and things picked up considerable speed as the foreign pre-sale buyers were sending in checks for between 10 to 20 percent of their contracts.

What I didn't know was just how many *deals* were being made. I was subsequently to learn (one year later), from just one private investor, that they had given Kodiak nearly a half-million for certain S.I.S. rights and because they were told it was money needed to help keep Mr. Wahl in place. (That deal produced many more questions and headaches than results.)

As the third American Film Market came around, we had posters and advertising running around the world in the trade papers with Moxey, Wahl, Davi, and Cattrall. More deposits were taken. . . . And then things began to fall apart.

Out of the clear, Mr. Wahl changed his mind about playing the lead, saying something about not wanting to play another cop. Talk about going crazy—this was a new one for me. In all my years I had never heard of an actor committing to the lead, signing a contract, taking money upfront, giving us permission to sell the package around the world, and then, nearly four months after the world had been sold on the picture with *him* in it . . . changing his mind.

His manager, Mr. Bloom, suddenly became inaccessible on the phone, and claimed he had no control over his client. (This was at least one fact that turned out to be true.) I tried to salvage the picture, but Bloom could dodge phone calls better than anyone I've ever met. The whole worldwide package was falling apart.

It was simply incomprehensible to Schmidt and me that our contractually committed lead had suddenly refused to live up to his contract. For Schmidt it was even tougher, because he'd collected quite a few dollars, lire, pounds, and yen on promises and start dates that we no longer could keep.

The "package," with Bloom, had turned out to contain a bomb and was a disaster that meant making dozens of phone calls to keep the financing in place. Even today, examining the particulars of what happened back then is painful.

At this point, there had been a succession of proposed starting dates, and the picture's budget in that first year with Kodiak Films had been everywhere from $1.5 million to $3.5 million. I had talked to more casting people, production people, and agents than I can possibly recall. The stop-go-stop word around town was that the picture was completely screwed up and would never be made. Our credibility and the town's perception of *Stainless Steel* was rusty, at best.

I recall, with some anger, that our first trying to get a deal set with Mr. Bloom and Ken Wahl turned out to be easy compared to trying to get our money back. Although Mr. Davi and Ms. Cattrall's options expired and they were entitled to keep their advances, Wahl and Bloom had not fulfilled their contracts. It wasn't until a lawsuit had been prepared and served against Mr. Bloom that a refund from Wahl showed up. Meanwhile, Bloom claimed poverty and asked that he be allowed to send his advance back in installments. (I'm surprised he didn't ask to make the payments with credit cards.)

For all the big talk about how lucky we were to have had Ken Wahl, in the few meetings we did have I personally found him incredibly difficult to work with.

His pulling out of the movie at that time seemed, to us, a near-fatal blow. However, when Wahl's big picture, *The Taking of Beverly Hills*, opened soon thereafter across the country and sank out of sight faster than the *Titanic*, my perception of our bad luck changed and I figured we'd been saved when he bailed out on us.

At the time, Mr. Schmidt somehow kept the other wolves at bay around the world, although nasty faxes started coming in from people who wanted their deposits back. But then Schmidt caught me by surprise when he decided he wasn't satisfied with the script and went off to secretly hire his own group to work on it. As the writer/producer, I was shocked to learn subsequently from my supposed Executive Producer partner that he had done so without even a word to me. Contractually, he didn't need my permission, but it made little to no sense to work that way. *I* certainly wasn't used to this type of secrecy. I was perplexed; and it was a feeling I would have again.

At the same time, the world market for what was selling and getting financed in our picture's genre (action-thriller) was changing, and our project suddenly appeared too low-budgeted and cheap to get financed. True or not, this perception by those putting up the money was what counted, and that meant raising the budget in order to go for it and pay bigger stars. That also sadly meant telling the director, Mr. Moxey, that the picture's escalated budget could no longer be financed without having a bigger and more internationally known theatrical name at the helm. So Mr. Moxey, who had put in countless hours, was now notified that he was out. He promptly told us that if the picture ever did get made, he had a pay-or-play contract—meaning he would have to be paid. Or so he and I thought.

By that time, I had accumulated cabinet files full of documents relating to the movie. I had put together dozens of casting lists, directors lists, crew lists, budgets, et al. In fact, I had so many budgets on file that no matter what was needed, I could pull one out at any price.

Frankly, I was getting embarrassed when I'd call some of my agent friends since they had had these calls from me before. In fact, I wondered if we were both wasting our time talking.

Enter Mr. Mike Wise, a longtime agent who had been referred to Mr. Schmidt and was now brought on board to see whether we could get the process of "packaging" the picture back together. Within a relatively brief time he had a script in director William Friedkin's hands. Mr. Friedkin had directed a number of big films, including two that had won six Academy Awards between them: *The French Connection* and *The Exorcist*. He liked the script, and within weeks a deal had been negotiated and we were sitting together discussing casting.

Mr. Schmidt went back to the fax machines and international phone calls, upping the sales prices around the world. He had to: We were now masters of a $10 million-dollar film.

However, Friedkin's one concern about a weakness in the script was suddenly shared by all. At the same time, it was also obvious I had done my last rewrite. After fifteen or so attempts at a final draft, I was burned out. That was when Mr. Bloom resurfaced and managed to come up with an idea that actually worked. He recommended a writer/client named Robert Boris, and when Boris showed up he brought new blood and talent to the process.

His new draft markedly improved my efforts to date. Everyone seemed pleased, and we sent the script out to stars under Mike Wise's consultation with million- to two-million-dollar offers attached. It was after we got our fifth major star turndown that Mr. Friedkin started having second thoughts on the validity of one of the lead roles, as written. His doubts were not shared by the rest of us, and even Schmidt was not interested in further script changes. And so, Mr. Friedkin bowed out. A friendly parting, but tough nonetheless. We had wanted to work with him.

In the previous fourteen months, we had notified the foreign buyers around the world by phone and fax that: The picture was a low-budget go at $1.5 million, then that it was $3.5 million and Moxey was in, and then that Wahl, Davi, and Cattrell were in. Then, that Wahl was out; then, that they were all out. Then, that Friedkin was in and the picture was going up to a budget of $10 million and we were going after the likes of Kurt Russell and Willem Dafoe. And finally, that they (the foreign investors) weren't to worry. So . . . to then call and fax them that Friedkin was now gone wasn't easy.

When we parted ways with William Friedkin, new (lower) budgets were requested, and I, along with Mike Wise, pulled together another directors list.

This was a level of wheel-spinning I had never encountered in my career. It was more like wheels within wheels, as the picture, now titled simply "S.I.S.," had already seen more than its fair share of ups and downs.

We decided to put out the latest script to the majors and mini-majors in hopes of attracting a domestic partner, but no one was biting. The only ones biting were the foreign investors/distributors, who wondered how many months (now going on eighteen at Kodiak, plus an additional two years on my own) it was going to take to get this picture off the ground.

Next in the director's door was Mark Lester. He was number four, to be exact, and was an accomplished journeyman known for action skills and the international success of his Arnold Schwarzenegger picture, *Commando*.

Doubts about the script suddenly resurfaced and Robert Boris was asked once again to do another set of changes. He, too, was approaching writer's burnout. He certainly had my sympathy. We continued debating ideas and changes that each of us wanted to see and, seemingly, no matter what Boris wrote, I wound up making more changes based on what Schmidt, Lester, Wise, and I found was needed.

More than any other time, it was at this juncture that I felt we were traveling in concentric circles and going absolutely nowhere. With Friedkin out, the budget hovered between $4 million and $7 million, depending on what day of the week it was, who you were talking to, and what the mood at Kodiak dictated.

Somehow, Mike Wise got us to focus on Lou Diamond Phillips for the lead, Detective Powers, and things started suddenly to come back together. Once Lou committed and a deal was struck, we went back to my original first choice of Scott Glenn for the role of Detective Vaughn. (This was actually the second submission to him, the first had been given nearly a year earlier.)

Scott liked what he read this time—and the idea of working with Lou Diamond Phillips. After meeting Mark Lester, he was comfortable enough with the group to commit. Within weeks we had a deal with his agent and we had the top two starring roles cast . . . again.

Within a few more weeks, we zeroed in on Chelsea Field to play the female lead, Kelly, after auditioning a dozen actresses. We screened her recent picture, *The Last Boy Scout*, wherein she had played the wife of Bruce Willis. Chelsea had a unique set of qualifications that fit the part: She was strong enough to stand up to Scott Glenn, smart enough to play a tough reporter, sexy enough to be an interesting love mate for Lou Diamond Phillips, and she was a terrific actress. Interestingly enough, by this time the combo of male stars, script, and director had four very well known female stars competing against her and willing to take enormous cuts in their established fees if it would help them land the role. Agents who had recently avoided my calls were now clamoring to get their actresses in to read for the female lead in the picture.

The power combination of Phillips and Glenn, and respect for their work, made for a complete change of venue around Kodiak Films. Spirits definitely perked up. The two leads were both internationally recognizable and respected talents. In fact, at the just-concluded Academy Awards, three of the winners from *Silence of the Lambs* had thanked Scott Glenn for his contributions to the film.

Scott's film career had included other major roles in *The Hunt for Red October*, *Backdraft*, *Urban Cowboy*, and *The Right Stuff*. Lou Diamond Phillips had gotten on the fast track with *La Bamba* and *Young Guns*; he also had a strong following among America's younger generation. The two male stars made for a team with great potential.

However, the pressure at that precise time on Mr. Schmidt to keep his company afloat was growing, and the cash drain to keep everything in place was mounting precipitously. Once a start date for the picture had been selected, we had a finite number of days in which to close all the foreign deals with these elements (stars/director) in place and get a domestic distribution deal. And then we had to bring it all to the banks, which in turn were to loan us the money against all the contracts. And once again, everything started to fall apart.

The investors who had forked over nearly half a million wanted their money back—now. A leading English distributor who had anted-up $60,000 in advances a year earlier wanted his money back. A major Japanese player wanted their money back. In addition, the company bonding our picture couldn't get an answer from Lloyd's of London, which normally backed it up. It was very simple: No bond, no money ... no movie.

I began getting a daily barrage of agent calls from the respective stars' emissaries saying they were worried. (They weren't the only ones.) Was the money in place for the film? Was Kodiak going out of business? Were we really starting the movie this time?

The fact was, though not privy to Kodiak's internal financing, it was a small office and you couldn't help but be aware we were often a step away from going belly-up as the cash flow was moment-to-moment and at times nonexistent. As one starting date was set, it was broken, and then another was set, and then another. We would hire production people on a Monday to start the following week, and before they were able to get going they'd get calls putting the process off. Some unfortunate crew people had to play this game with us for months, and then just couldn't take it any longer.

Scott Glenn's agent put the pressure on us, big-time, to protect him and demanded and got more money to hold him in place. Lou Diamond Phillips' agent and lawyer were all over us to "get real" or they were pulling out. (On the other hand, Lou and Scott seemed willing to do whatever they could to make it all happen.) The director's agent was calling, too, to find out what the hell was going on? All of their contracts were reaching the critical-mass stage of either getting paid in full or losing our upfront deposits of several hundred thousand dollars, along with their commitments. I remember that this was the third film package to be advertised at the AFM, and that every time I put up a poster in my office that showed the name of the movie, the director, and its stars the whole thing was changed. I was beginning to get superstitious.

Simultaneously, the bank got down to real business and went through twenty-two foreign sales contracts with a fine-tooth comb. Each change they required meant a flurry of worldwide faxes to correct or revise the contractual language. To keep up with the start dates required, we moved into "official" pre-production: a time period wherein you hire the rest of your cast and crew, scout locations, and start fine-tuning the production.

It was at this time that everyone once again agreed that the script needed more work even though Boris and I had fried our collective brains over revisions and, between us, could put a stack of changes that piled nearly five feet high off the floor. Actually, as with budgets, we had so many different versions that any new idea mentioned could actually be found somewhere within one of the older scripts, although there were so many scripts to look through that it was easier to go and write something new.

Nonetheless, a new voice was added to the scripting chorus, that being Michael Krohn, who in one week actually made incredible breakthroughs and helped elevate the dialogue to another plane. With no time left for mistakes, he was asked to work out of our offices and every few hours was with the director and I going over the latest changes.

However, Mr. Schmidt's luck and my own had finally started to run out. The convergence of the stars' agents, their attorneys, other attorneys representing outside investors, and more pressure from foreign funders—coupled with the enormous cash flow demands—was in real danger of sinking the ship, once and for all.

The final process of adjusting everyone's contracts to reflect all the current status quos and changed dates, plus having to carry fifteen people who were now prepping the show, together with further last-minute changes that were being required by a new bond company, and a new insurance company . . . all added up to a window that was going to shut like a guillotine on our necks.

What's more, Kodiak's ongoing depositions and lawsuits facing them on other matters made it all the more difficult, and even Mr. Schmidt was feeling the effects of the pressure. (Within weeks he would be in the hospital.)

In May and June 1992 it got worse. Much worse. The agents stood in line to see which one was going to be the first to push his client out the door, whereas Scott and Lou were beginning to look pensive, although they managed to stay upbeat. However, the technical people who had been brought on the picture and were using our offices were getting crazed. The location manager, one of the first people to get hired in the pre-production phase, had been on staff so long, due to the pushed-start dates, that he'd found enough locations for three movies. The production designer we had at the time got edgy and we began having personality clashes. The end result was his release from the film, and a new man was brought on to pick up the ball. The production coordinator was now entrenched, as well as the first and second assistant directors and the director of photography. A massive calendar board was put up on a wall with the day-to-day shooting schedule laid down in (erasable) marker. The production was beginning to feel very, very pregnant and the labor pains were obviously taking their toll.

The budget had found its own level of nearly $7 million, while the number of shooting days was projected at forty. This included six-day work weeks with twelve-hour days as part of our schedule for principal photography. Twenty-page computer budgets with up to fifty categories a page were being done daily, sometimes two in a day. Casting agents were being interviewed. Foreign investors were having their collective hands held by fax, around the world. It looked as if we were about to start the movie.

And then, once again, it began to unravel.

We had put off the starting date four times within the past six weeks. The weekly overhead had zoomed upwards into tens of thousands of dollars for a payday that rolled around every two weeks. The two stars were getting other film offers that conflicted with our schedule, and if we pushed our start date back any further we'd lose them. Schmidt was forced to come up with hundreds of thousands in cash to keep it all together. The bank was throwing last-minute language changes at us that required new revisions in the existing foreign-sales contracts. Negotiations with the new bond company indicated we were going to have to pay out and allow for hundreds of thousands in new production costs that we felt were not needed. The insurance companies were balking at giving us insurance because the picture was inspired by a real unit of the L.A.P.D. The production costs were again revised because of the yearly increase in Screen Actor's Guild fees, plus higher extras' fees going into effect just as we were starting the picture. Rising costs having to do with maintaining all the pre-production people on staff for an extended period were calculated into the equation. The Director's Guild called to tell us Mr. Moxey had asked them to step in and make sure he got paid before we started shooting; they told us, point-blank, that either he got paid or they would yank all their other members off our current crew. The outside investor who had put up a half-million in cash filed a lien against the company, effectively blocking the entire picture unless Schmidt could come to terms with them.

"Terms" was the wrong word. It was "war," as these two wouldn't even talk to each other. I suddenly became an intermediary between them, and while Schmidt battled the international problems and kept the ship afloat, I worked the creative side, trying to keep all the players from bolting.

The stars' and co-star's lawyers, agents, publicists, and associates at their respective agencies couldn't believe we were going to pull it off, and the fact was, each of them only had a portion of the bad news. Rumors about the production's collapse were moving around town faster than phone calls to try and offset them.

Then, Mr. Schmidt dropped another bomb on the production side when he told us, categorically, that he couldn't raise enough money for us to shoot for forty days.

The director couldn't believe the new mandate: that we shoot it all in thirty-four. He no longer had a chance to digest that when the boom was lowered again, three days later, and we were told to cut the shooting days down to twenty-eight, and then in the same day down even further. If we couldn't raise more money, then we had to make do on less.

After working on an endless succession of scripts, the question was no longer one of plot lines but of how to shoot a forty-day movie in less than twenty-eight. It literally meant ripping pages out of the script: cutting scenes, cutting dialogue, cutting extras. It meant cutting anything that wasn't contractually required by law or required by the forces of nature, such as film stock and cameras. It meant more and tighter budgets. It meant a director who had reached the end of his own patience and was threatening to leave the film. The time period between harried calls from agents, production supply houses, and crew members was getting shorter and shorter. Without money, we were going to hit the wall en masse. I saw the headlines in the trades: "Production Company Commits Suicide!" It was going to be the Hollywood version of Guyana's Jim Jones massacre.

Instead, the core group pushed, pulled, cajoled, begged, pleaded, promised, and swore to all who would listen that we could keep moving and that this special project was going to be worth all our extra efforts.

And then it all got worse: The bond company's analysis of our budget showed it to be too tight again and we had to adjust our numbers upwards. The insurance company needed more expensive coverage, the bank charges were going to be higher than projected, the contingency fund was going to have to be raised. It all added to another $450,000 above what we had calculated just a week before. And there was no way to raise any more money.

At that point, I suggested we ask the three most expensive elements in the "package" to defer parts of their salaries. Schmidt laughed when I proposed the idea, and almost made me a side bet I couldn't do it.

The first one I called was Lou Diamond Phillips. I said I needed to see him right away but didn't say why. Within hours, I was at his home asking him to effectively defer a substantial six-figure sum. Without consulting with his agent or lawyer, without asking for something else in return, without making me promise him anything in exchange, he agreed on the spot. Two other individuals did the same. Hope was once again revived, although we were fast approaching Black Thursday, a day only one week away—a day which all involved knew to be the very last second we could get the picture going or be forced to declare bankruptcy.

But even Lou's deferral did not compensate for the fact that there was no more money to pay the pre-production people, no more that could be advanced to the other stars, to the lawyers—no more to anyone. The only thing left to do was to cut the shooting schedule down again! Drop it from twenty-eight days to twenty-five. That meant more budgets and had the director, myself, the production manager, the location manager, and related assistants staring at the big production board in unison, for when you get that close to starting a movie, it is all inextricably woven together like a three-dimensional puzzle with a thousand parts. Move any one of them and they all jiggle.

Once you get this close to starting, your options become fewer and fewer. And yet, out of necessity we either had to move forward and bring on a casting director and immediately start casting all the other fifty speaking parts in the movie, or when we did start (in ten days) we would be without a cast. It didn't seem as if things could get any dicier, but they did. We scheduled our first full day of casting for that Thursday afternoon. It was the same afternoon as the start of the Los Angeles riots, and for those actors who showed up it was truly a memorable occasion. (We tried to reach their agents to cancel the meetings but they had already left their offices for their homes—to defend them in case of attack.) Actors had come across town dodging racing fire engines and police cars. They had taken circuitous routes in order to avoid being shot at or mugged. Together, we looked out from the Kodiak offices as smoke started to drift across town from the early fires that were being set.

$700 million dollars' worth of property was about to go up in smoke, fed by hundreds of fires throughout the city. The reaction to the Rodney King verdict was going to be unprecedented. It was the beginning of the most destructive urban rioting in the history of the nation. The actors who came in to read that Thursday afternoon for the supporting parts of the S.I.S. unit were wired. They literally bounced off the walls. After just a few minutes, I had to have the casting people tell the actors ahead of time to quit slamming the huge glass tabletop in the board room or it was going to be a two thousand-dollar audition for them.

The parts we chose to have them read were high-voltage, emotional scenes. One particular actor who came in to read for the part of one of the bank robbers went wild and blew us away, along with the coffee on the tables, which went flying. It was four days of casting that were supercharged, whereas outside, the city was in near-anarchy.

The topper for the end of the week came when our

computer finally blew up from having to do so many budgets. In turn, the director blew up from having his original forty-day schedule crucified down to a paltry twenty-five. He claimed, and was right when he said it, that TV movies had more time to shoot. He started calling his lawyer and his agent to get him out of the picture in between our casting sessions.

Even Schmidt no longer believed we could make it happen. Bankruptcy was heading our way. He fielded call after call from an army of lawyers who, each, were demanding last-second changes in their respective clients' deals. His own lawyer was telling me privately that the agreements could not be done by next Thursday and that it was not a realistic closing date; he said the paperwork could not be drafted and put in order, and that the five primary people involved could not agree in time to save the production, or Kodiak as a company.

We desperately needed hundreds of thousands more than we had, no matter how we figured it. Schmidt placed calls around the world looking for money, and the second he thought he found some he put the head of his sales department on a flight to Europe.

She had ten minutes to pack before she headed for Paris and Madrid. She flew ten thousand miles without even having a firm appointment or knowing where the two potential investors/distributors could be found. It was all in hopes she could locate the French and Spanish buyers somewhere in Paris and Madrid and get them to sign contracts for their territories: These were contracts we desperately needed to run back to the bank in Los Angeles and help salvage the film by providing more money. She had forty-eight hours to do it in, and she did it.

Nevertheless, it still wasn't enough. We were told to cut the budget again, but this time we flat-out refused. There was nothing left to cut: no days, no people, no scenes. The script had gone from 110 pages down to just 94 in ten days. As it was, I, along with Robert Boris and the director, were already having second thoughts about cuts we'd just made. To work for four years to get a final, so-called best script and then have it decimated was unbelievable to all of us. The movie had been pregnant for longer than an elephant, and now that the baby was due we collectively had to amputate its limbs; and yet ... at the last minute we worked together and figured out how to say it all in 16 fewer pages.

In the final twenty-four hours before all the parties involved were scheduled to assemble for the sacred "closing ceremony" on Black Thursday, I physically stopped the director from walking out the door — twice. The second time I handed him a quickly typed letter I'd made up that said he had exactly fifteen minutes to sign off on the budget and stay with us, or we might sue him from here to kingdom come. (Legally, he probably didn't have to sign anything, but he did, thank God.)

With less than twenty-four hours to go, Wolf Schmidt got so fed up with everyone's last-minute demands that he finally acknowledged defeat and gave up. (In two years I had never seen this man give up on anything.) I stood in his office as he called in the production manager and gave Matt Hintlian orders to fire everyone in sight. It was all over, there was no money left for the week's payroll, no money to make the movie, no nothing. It was over. He had pulled every rabbit out of his hat that existed and then some.

I walked out, following right behind Matt, and pulled him into my own office. Shutting the door, I told him to forget what he'd just been told and that I could get Schmidt to go one more step. I told Matt that everyone at the moment was out of the office scouting locations or doing other production business, so a few more hours didn't matter. He agreed to disobey the boss, figuring, like me, that there was nothing to lose. I had nearly four years invested and would not give up until someone threw me bodily out of the joint.

That night, I knew this had to be it, one way or the other. I was stressed out myself and wanted a resolution. Physically, I found the pressure had finally gotten to me. I had lost seven pounds in as many days. At this rate, we had to close the deal or I figured I would simply disappear.

The next morning was Thursday, D-day. We either close the deal or close the doors. After another sleepless night, I was at the office before eight, and at 9 A.M. a tentative time to meet had still not been set. Schmidt's primary lawyer told me again, an hour later, that "just willing it to happen wasn't going to make it happen," as there were far too many loose ends and the paperwork still wasn't ready. At 11 A.M. Schmidt and I met and he said the same thing: It wasn't happening, it was over.

I refused to let him cancel the meeting, and told him that if we could get everyone in one room we at least had a chance to pull it all together. We had to try. Everyone involved had from months to years of work at stake, and besides, it looked as if his company would have to go bankrupt if it *didn't* happen. What was more, if we quit now, we'd never know if we could have done it. He agreed. At 11:30 he got on the phone and started swearing. He categorically demanded that all the respective lawyers and principals meet at 12:30 in the Century City law offices of the bond company. People bitched and squawked and said it was a waste of time, but he wouldn't take no for an answer. We were all to meet in an hour *or else*.

At 12:30, I walked into one of the oldest law firms in the country. They had allocated their biggest conference room, plus three other smaller ones for side meetings. They even had three legal secretaries on standby to do last-minute changes. Upon entering the conference room I literally began to laugh. In front of me an enormous, oval-shaped table stretched twenty-two feet in length, and on it in metal binders like an extended accordion were contracts and documents that went from one end of the table to the other and then spilled over onto the floor. There were something like eighty-one different documents, each one anywhere from 5 to 50 or more pages in length, and each one xeroxed in sets of six. It was, by all accounts, the largest group of documents for a "closing signing" that anyone participating had ever seen. The documents represented individual contracts from twenty-three countries around the world, plus all the interlocutory documents between the insurance company, the bond company, the production company, the foreign-sales company, the domestic distributor, the bank, the people who filed a lawsuit over the $500,000, two production company subsidiaries, my company, plus the stars' revised contracts and all the other related documents and their addendums. In total, it was actually laughable.

By 1:30, I started counting heads and came up with fourteen people, half of whom were lawyers. It was at that point that we all started to negotiate with each other over the final terms, conditions, and definitions of all that lay before us. What happened over the next eleven straight hours is still a blur but involved an endless series of side-bar meetings between various groups. On at least three different occasions everything came to a halt.

By six o'clock that night, it became apparent that even though we weren't close to finalizing anything, the reality was that unless we began physically to sign all the documents, it would never end. A daisy chain of four of us lined up and started signing documents that were passed down from one to the other, while several others looked over our shoulders to make sure it all kept moving.

Hands started to cramp up. Pens ran out of ink. Our signatures became completely illegible. In between signings, other lawyers would enter with redrafted and re-negotiated new documents, and certain groups would exit to argue in side rooms or discuss the latest proposals. The physical signing was interrupted so many times it lasted for three hours and didn't end until nine that night. Dinner was sent in.

There was just enough time to focus on the last few details. The head of the banking group swore he had

Frank Sacks

gone this far and wasn't leaving until it was done.

Schmidt called me aside for a private meeting to tell me the number-one problem remaining was the fact we still didn't have enough money to make the movie. Number two was that the group who wanted their $500,000 back were really putting it to him and making new last-second demands.

At that critical point, he convinced me the only way to make up for the needed cash was for me to delay taking my producer's fees and put the money toward the production. In other words, either I could let the whole thing fall apart, or let it go forward and not get paid. . . . It was my decision. I now added my own name to a list that included three others who had agreed to put part of their fees back into the film. (It is simply amazing what people will do to make a movie.)

Unfortunately, I had long planned on the money I'd had coming—like for two years—and couldn't tell whether Schmidt was bluffing. That is, if I didn't agree, would he somehow miraculously come up with the difference out of his own pocket? (I'll never know.) What I did know was that over the previous month I had seen him scrambling to get every cent he could to make the movie, and had been told he'd even put up his house in Malibu as collateral. I figured in my own mind that if I refused and he wasn't bluffing, the whole thing would explode in my face at the eleventh hour. I gave in and agreed to delay taking any money. (It turned out to be a financial hardship that was to cause incredible problems for my family, but the alternative was no money *and* no movie .)

The number-two problem remaining was the intractable position that the group with $500,000 already invested had taken. I called the principals involved aside and went into two different meetings with them to convince them to bend a little in order to have something as opposed to nothing if they refused. They refused.

This eleventh-hour stalemate stopped it all. People were speechless, since it seemed the only thing left to say was good night.

I left it all behind me and started walking down the long hallways of the law firm. Their offices took up the entire floor and I was able to walk half a block before coming to a corner in one of the Century City Tower buildings. Making two full circuits of the entire floor, I prayed as I walked that God would now intervene. I had done everything I could, and it was now or never.

At two minutes to midnight, after I'd gone back inside, it finally happened. We all agreed to agree, and finalized the production financing for the picture. Millions of dollars had been secured to make the movie. Four years of work was about to pay off. Over five million in cash would be transferred within twenty-four hours into our account so that the following day we could begin spending in order to start the picture in five more days, on July 8.

I had five days to get the sets built, officially hire nearly a 150 people, gather two hundred tons of trucks and equipment, and start the movie. We did it.

The real problems were about to begin. . . .

ACT II

On Wednesday morning, the first day of the movie, I awoke at dawn to a heavy rain. It was the first day in one hundred years that it had rained on a July 8 in Los Angeles! I couldn't believe it . . . .

As I drove on the freeway, watching my windshield wipers (on high) trying to keep the glass clear, I was a mixed bag of emotions. Here we were on Day One about to go over schedule. We had over five script pages to shoot in a barbecue scene involving all the members of the S.I.S. I had to start thinking about how to rewrite it so that we could shoot indoors if need be.

Heading for the location, I should have been feeling ten feet off the ground, but the prospect of not getting paid for at least the next six months or for the last two years of work was having a major impact on my family. It was a tough pill to swallow, but I was fortunate enough to be producing what I hoped would become a movie worth all our efforts.

As I got closer to the location, the rain subsided and my hopes began to rise. Normally, the first day of shooting is one of the toughest. A movie crew and its cast have to work like a unit or you have problems, major problems. Putting over a hundred people together who have never worked as a team before takes two or three days to shake out the wrinkles. Knowing this upfront, production managers keep the first day or two light. On average, you shoot three pages of your script in one twelve-hour day. Our schedule permitted no such luxury. It was five pages and then some--on Day One.

What got us through that day on time was largely the result of the fact we had all been together at a party Lou Diamond Phillips had thrown at his house over the weekend. He had invited the entire cast, crew, and their favorite others to his place to break the ice. We danced, talked, introduced ourselves to each other, and partied. It was indicative of Lou's one-of-a-kind style.

However, though we had moved into high gear overnight, the real production problems were surfacing early. First up, a call came from the Screen Actor's Guild notifying me that as Kodiak owed money from prior business, we had to make good on the SAG account or they would shut us down on the new movie by the end of the day. With six minutes to spare that night, a check was cleared by their office.

Next, I had simultaneous demands from Lou's, Scott's, and the director's agents that all monies due each of them be immediately placed into separate escrow accounts. Again, an unusual request. But rumors of the production company's financial status had them all worried. Their last-minute contract changes granted such demands and we had no choice. Agreeing to it was one thing; getting the bank, the agents, the lawyers, and the Guild to agree on the exact terms was another. But it was done.

And, although over a million dollars was going straight from the bank to their escrow accounts, I was having trouble getting three hundred dollars to the transportation department for gas money on the set--a fact I didn't understand. The escrow monies were wholly separate from the $750,000 that had just gone into the production account with Wells Fargo Bank. So what happened?

When you move two city blocks of trucks and equipment, including portable bathrooms, dressing rooms, production offices, lighting and camera trucks, etc., it requires a good deal of plain, ordinary cash in addition to everyone's weekly or daily paychecks.

Upon placing calls to the production office, the word from the production accountant was threefold: (A) Production didn't know we needed the money; (B) They were so busy it had been overlooked; and (C) They couldn't find the written requests we'd given them days earlier.

Instincts told me none of the above was the correct answer, and I expressed my concern to the production manager because he was the financial coordinator between the set and the production accountant. He was less than happy with the news. What it meant, among other things, was having to walk up to Scott Glenn on Day One and apologize to him personally for not having the cash to pay his "per diem" (money for his hotel and food bills for the week), as contractually stipulated. It was not my idea of a way to build his confidence in the production. And though for some it may seem no big deal, an actor's "per diem" is one of the little things in life that counts more than the amount of money involved. It is a basic courtesy and not something you screw up by overlooking or making excuses about, especially not on the first day of shooting.

Next up was the fact we had taken elaborate and

secret precautions to not disclose the name of our film, *S.I.S.* (in order to avoid any possible conflicts or problems with the police). We were hyper-sensitive about making a movie about this secret unit. Somehow, knowledge of the film found its way into the offices of the *Hollywood Reporter*. They called Schmidt and we pleaded with them not to run the story. They informed us that they were running it with or without our comments. On Wednesday morning we were all reading the Page One story. In turn, of course, everyone in town had now been alerted to what we were doing.

However, we still didn't make it easy for anyone to find us, and used a cover name of "The Arica Project" to hide our tracks as well as possible. All the trucks, call sheets, and signs showing directions to our locations, and all printed matter, carried the Arica name. This game plan of secrecy had been worked on for some time because of what we all felt was the extremely sensitive subject of our movie, the S.I.S. itself.

In fact, our penchant for secrecy carried nearly all the way through to the end of the production. However, when the City of Los Angeles finally found out we had called the film something other than "S.I.S.," I received a letter of reprimand from the city's film office. (Perhaps the idea may be unjustifiable, but I wondered whether we'd really have been given permission by City Hall to shoot if they'd known upfront what the film was all about.) Between the facts and fiction surrounding the S.I.S. over the years, it seemed a prudent move on our part not to broadcast our intentions. What seemed a little crazy in the end was the decision to not pass out until the last week a hundred baseball caps emblazoned with the letters "S.I.S." on them; these were the kind of traditional items you gave to your cast and crew. Funny enough, once they did get them, the cast and crew seemed so sensitive to the S.I.S. that only two people had their hats on the following day. (To this day, very few of them wear them in public.) They're true collector's items, especially because the film's name was finally changed to *Extreme Justice*, after the S.I.S. title was researched and tested out last out of fourteen choices.

From the first day in September 1988 when I conceived the idea of making a movie inspired by the S.I.S., I always looked at it as a subject that would be controversial, and therefore marketable as a film. And though no one, to my knowledge, in four years of research had evidence to show the S.I.S. as anything other than a highly volatile topic, it was a hot potato.

From the beginning, I knew it could at least be a movie that would get people thinking. In the four years of working on a script, a key problem was how to tell a story about them without condemning the entire unit. I never really wanted to condemn them, but realized that any film about them would become explosive and controversial if you went for a reality-based picture. The premeditated-hunter aspect of what they do added in a scare factor that heightened their violence even more. The fact is, nevertheless, I always believed that half the audience would be on the side of the S.I.S., no matter what was scripted. I knew it had to be balanced, so this was a far more difficult scripting task than I ever imagined.

In addition, just like the audience that would judge the S.I.S. and the film, those who contributed to the film brought their own attitudes to bear on the end result. Overall, it was and has been that rare chance to at least make a movie about something real.

Within days of the *Hollywood Reporter*'s disclosure of our film, my life off the set began to get nerve-wracking on its own. Within just twenty-four hours, I was having serious problems with my home phone. Every time I started talking with someone about what I felt was confidential information regarding the S.I.S., or the movie, the damn phone line would "click." Over the following weeks it happened over and over again. Even more frustrating was the fact that on four separate occasions the click was immediately followed by a total disconnection from the person on the other end. I called the phone company on several occasions, and although they looked into the matter and twice sent out a field repairman, they never found anything wrong. They even replaced old equipment on the chance that it might have been causing the problem. It wasn't. The phone interruptions continued, as did the timely clicking noise that always coincided with my talking about the S.I.S.

It was at that time I was told by Stephen Yagman (the S.I.S.-prosecuting attorney referred to in Part I of this book) that the FBI was conducting its own investigation of the S.I.S. I seriously thought there might be a connection between my phone problems and their ongoing investigation. Other events soon occurred to make me a lot more suspicious.

The trade article had also triggered an immediate inspection by a city official of our permits and equipment. An unannounced inspector showed up from a city department and walked onto our set without notifying anyone he was present. (Normal protocol is to contact a production executive and let him know the inspector is there for an inspection.) This guy walked onto the set, found two ungrounded fuse boxes, and headed to the electrical generator to pull the plug himself. The electrical man in charge caught him in the act and nearly punched his own lights out!

We had five miles of electrical cable strung out over three buildings and thousands of square feet. It covered six sets on three different floors in a former-hospital location known as Lakeview Terrace. Once our production manager was told about the visitor, he calmed things down and immediately set about correcting the problem. The official from the city issued us a warning and disappeared.

On the third day of shooting, I was notified by the Director's Guild of America that we had twenty-four hours to either agree to settle with Mr. Moxey or they were going to pull their own plug by removing other Guild members off our film, including our current director and his entire DGA crew. The surprise here was that Mr. Schmidt had told all concerned at the closing that he had taken care of this $50,000 matter a week before.

In fact, he'd included the amount in money that had been deducted in figuring the budget at the closing. Once notified of the DGA demands, he told us it had been a mix-up between him and his in-house financial man, and he had assumed it had already been paid. An agreement followed with the DGA after a flurry of faxes, calls, and letters were transmitted, and Mr. Moxey was then paid.

Amazingly enough, problems or not, by the end of the third day we were a half-day ahead of schedule. Director Mark Lester was doing an average of only three or four takes per shot. The director of photography, Mark Irwin, was lighting and moving the camera to a new setup faster than you could catch him doing it.

The extra half-day allowed us to throw back into the script an important cemetery scene, if only we could find the right one on a moment's notice. It all happened so fast that Chelsea Field, our key actress, was not notified of the change until the last minute. The fact that it was a new scene between her and Lou, with extensive new dialogue, came as a real shock. I remember watching her anxiously head toward her trailer to memorize her lines, with an hour to go before we would shoot them.

On this picture all the actors were under pressure to be on their marks at all times. As a director, Lester's forte was action, but though we had plenty of action, it was a script requiring dramatic performances from every single individual with a speaking line. There were no throwaway parts.

For me, it was near-serendipity that we had actors who could do it all on one or two takes, coupled with a director who could get in thirty or more setups a day. There was very little time for direction of the talent. Rehearsals and blocking of the shots was done incredibly fast, and the actors were relied on to know what to do. During the first ten days of shooting, four different actors approached me and let me know that they appreciated the freedom to do their work but that they had more freedom than they could sometimes cope with.

The thing I couldn't cope with was the lack of money to take care of the bills. It made no sense to have been funded with millions of dollars and still not have enough money each day to take care of approved costs. And also, after all the preparation to get the show going, I couldn't get a proper accounting from the production accountant. After ten days, the only thing that showed up was a useless balance sheet that revealed nothing but zeros for expenditures to date.

I made repeated daily demands to the production accountant for an accounting, as did the production manager. He was obliged to pay the bills and catch up with the payment schedules as nothing was being done.

Within a few more days, things got so serious that there was nothing left to do but bring the problem directly to the attention of the bond company and my lawyer. On July 24, I called him in the middle of his vacation in Hawaii to express my own dire concern about the events taking place. I suspected we were missing a lot of money and I told him I had also immediately alerted the appropriate parties about the potential problem. Finally, I decided that the principals in control would find the answers and I had best concentrate on my own job of producing the movie.

Ten days later, the answers came in spades. An unauthorized series of wire transfers had been made from the production account and hundreds of thousands of dollars were missing. Within days, a series of important events occurred. First, the bond company notified me they were going to take over the picture unless things got straightened out very fast. Second, when I confronted a principal involved and asked him point-blank about it, he would not disclose how much money was transferred, where it went, or for what purpose. In fact, he got upset with me for bringing the matter to anyone else's attention. But I was very worried, and I wasn't the only one.

On July 31, 1992, the bond company sent a letter notifying the production company that they were taking over the "administration" of the picture.

Producing a movie with money is tough enough. Trying to produce it without money is problematic at best. It was a situation totally affecting *me*, but no one who knew the real answers would comment. (Only in the movie business can a problem like this occur and not make the roof fall in. When there are millions at stake in completing a picture, the people involved first turn their attention to finishing the picture, lest it all go down the drain.)

Soon thereafter, new agreements were formulated between the parties involved with regard to the matters in dispute.

While that confrontation had heated up, however, the action on the set managed to keep pace. (In retrospect, I am certain it took the combination of managing the set problems and not being a party to the missing production funds that kept me in position as the producer.)

On July 28, it was brought to my attention that a member of the real S.I.S. was watching us. Bill Lucking, who plays S.I.S. member Cusack on screen, was approached while we were working in Venice by a man who introduced himself as a veteran S.I.S. member. Bill later told me the fellow had shown some concern during their conversation when the S.I.S. man mentioned to him that part of our story apparently paralleled some of his own private life. If true, it was a coincidence, like two or three other unusual details that were written as fiction but turned out to be close to the truth.

Within two days, another individual claiming to be with the S.I.S. contacted Yaphet Kotto by phone. Before I could look into it, I was informed by a third party that a secret meeting had also taken place between my location manager and three members of the S.I.S., at their request.

To my surprise, upon confronting the location manager, Bill Doyle, with this fact, he confirmed it. When I asked him what the nature of their meeting had been, he declined to talk about it other than to say the S.I.S. members had questions about what we were doing. Well, if anybody had questions, I did. I wanted to know what they wanted with my location manager? I never found out.

As tensions over money continued to swirl around the set, the events on and off the set kept my attention balanced between the two. I will forever remember the next night on location at 5th and Broadway in downtown Los Angeles.

It was an all-night shoot that was to go from 7:00 P.M. to 7:00 A.M. and involved the entire Torres rape scene within the script. At approximately 10:00 P.M., two L.A.P.D. squad cars raced through the middle of our set with their lights flashing. They drove down an alley separating our parking from the area we were shooting. I was inside the 40-foot production trailer and their acceleration literally rocked it by the proximity of their high-speed chase. Seconds later, a police helicopter with a search beacon hovered overhead.

Although at first I figured that the cop cars were ours and part of the staging outside, I knew the helicopter was not in the budget and immediately went out to see what was happening.

As our "S.I.S." actors staged a major shootout on the set, real cops were, in effect, in full pursuit of someone else. Squad cars were suddenly all around us. But as quick as they all showed up, they were gone. It was the talk of the cast and crew for the next two hours. That is, until the real shooting started!

At just after 1:00 A.M., Yaphet Kotto and I were having a cup of coffee near his trailer. As we stood together, we both watched as another of the frequent neighborhood drug deals was going down not more than 150 feet away. As clear as if someone was talking to me, I heard a voice say: "Move away! These guys are going to start shooting!"

It was so clear in my mind that I expressed the exact same words to Yaphet out loud. It was a thought totally disconnected from the conversation we were having. And for whatever reason, we both immediately moved back toward the trailer. As Yaphet will attest to this day, within ten seconds the two guys we had been watching drew their guns and blew each other away!

Yaphet and I went into states of shock. The gunfire attracted about fifteen of our crew to the area. The police we'd hired to watch over us drew their own guns while the majority of others at the location assumed the shots were our own because the scenes we were filming around the corner involved hundreds of blank rounds being fired.

The last report I had was that the two shooters had gotten into an argument over a crack deal and at point-blank range decided to have it out. It was more than wild, it was scary.

That night and into the next day, Yaphet and I told the story about what had happened, but there were so many other things going on that our experience together was quickly replaced by other events to come.

ACT III

One of those events found us in the midst of more potential trouble, when the cast and crew showed up at the corner of 6th and Central for another all-night shoot. This time, to film the opening sequence to the movie wherein the S.I.S. watches a perp as he robs and kills a liquor store manager--and then faces the S.I.S. for the first and last time.

Always looking for realism, we had picked another locale that didn't need any set dressing to qualify for a hell hole surrounded by winos, drug dealers, and very dangerous people.

As I watched the crew set up the first shot, I was already nervous because we had extras and stars dressed precisely like the people all around us. Scott Glenn was covered in dirt and rags, and blended in so well the locals had no idea he wasn't one of them. In fact, a couple of the bums asked him how he had gotten into the movie? He told them it was luck and that he'd just been picked up off the street.

However, a couple of our female "bag lady" extras were being hustled by bums and needed to be kept in a van and away from the location until just moments before they were needed. It was crazy, to say the least. There was a complete blur between who was acting and who wasn't. In addition, the location had literally dozens of homeless transients moving all around us. And, though we had six motorcycle L.A.P.D. cops to watch the traffic and us, I told our production manager to get on the phone and get more help.

Unfortunately, the additional guards didn't show up in time and at 11:00 P.M. two of the street people standing within only a few feet of the crew got into a vicious knife fight. The loser staggered through the middle of the cast and crew, bleeding profusely from knife wounds in his chest. He had been repeatedly stabbed, and left a trail of blood on the sidewalk as he made his way through our midst. He stumbled only a few feet before collapsing on the street, while his attacker quickly fled on foot. In minutes, he was unconscious and was picked up by paramedics, who took him to a nearby hospital.

In one sense, it was impossible to distinguish which angle was reality and which way the cameras should be facing. The whole night was a paradox of trying to re-create the violent and hostile reality around us for the cameras in front of us. Luckily, we made it through the night without more problems.

As the show rolled forward, the events surrounding the action behind the scenes became something we shared in common and to that extent created a tighter bond among the cast and crew.

We were two-thirds of the way through our schedule when another potentially explosive element came into play: The Teamsters suddenly wanted to talk to me about our independent-production status and the fact that we had not employed any of their members. For the next ten days I talked with the union's chief production negotiator in order to try to reach a compromise about our independent "non-union" status. To some extent, they understood that our budget had dictated that we go with non-union crew members. However, in the end, I had to reach a compromise with them or risk a Teamsters picket line encircling our production.

As a show of good faith and respect for their people, we came to an understanding, although this wasn't easy to negotiate because the threat to shut us down was not idle talk. At the time I was talking and meeting with them, I couldn't predict the outcome, and quietly began to prepare for the worst. I put on retainer the best labor attorney I could find this side of Washington. Together, we made plans to file a court injunction against the Teamsters if the negotiations failed and their actions forced us to shut down. Thankfully, it never came to pass.

By the time we had filmed nearly three-quarters of the movie, people familiar with our problems felt we had been through a trial by fire. From my own perspective, I found that the work being done and the dedication of the cast and crew were overcoming all our other problems. It was the realization of a long-standing dream for me that their concentration and extra effort was showing up in the screening room every night. And though only a few of us could see the daily's, I didn't have to create any false sense of accomplishment for those on the set. Professionals know when it's working and when it's not. For me, those images going down on film were more than enough to keep my own spirits buoyed.

In looking back at the entire production experience there was, however, one day in particular that turns out to be the best example of an inside look at *Extreme Justice*.

It was actually an incredibly beautiful California day at the beach. We had planned to film a climactic action sequence involving the entire S.I.S. unit in a stakeout. The location was the busy Washington Boulevard area where it intersects with Venice beach. During the summer the entire area is jammed with hundreds of vendors selling everything from T-shirts to sunglasses. The day we showed up, the sidewalk was crowded with tens of thousands of locals and tourists who were cruising from Marina Del Ray to Santa Monica.

To cover the action we had an especially large crew and cast, including five camera teams standing by to shoot the stunts and action sequences, plus fifty extras in addition to a dozen principals: nearly 200 people in total.

The scene involved four young surfer types who attempt to hold up St. Mark's Bar. As the robbers exit the bar, they are met by the S.I.S. and all hell breaks loose. Two of the robbers hop in their Jeep and run over one of the squad members while the other two perps are chased through the crowds by Scott and Lou.

The action splits up as the two guys in the Jeep are trapped and get into a gunfight with the other S.I.S. members. The stunt driver in the Jeep then loses control after crashing through a dozen street stands, flips the vehicle upside down, and sends the other stunt man flying twenty feet through the air. He was supposed to land on the roof of an unmarked S.I.S. car. The difficulty was that all of this was to take place on the move with the shots being fired and the stunt men having gunshot explosions going off around them and on their bodies.

The Jeep flip was to take an hour to set up. Over three hours later, it finally happened. In the interim, several of the local vendors had gone to our bank to cash small checks we issued to cover their potential losses for the day, because we were filming in their area. The vendors returned enraged when the bank didn't have the few hundred dollars needed to make good on their checks. Within minutes the irate street vendors had gotten together and were threatening to start cracking heads and destroying our film equipment.

It was at this same time that Bill Lucking pulled me aside and told me about his just-concluded conversation with the real S.I.S. vet standing somewhere within the crowd around us.

As word had leaked to the news media about our film and the fact that we had been experiencing some rather unusual problems, we decided to capitalize on the situation. Our strategy to keep everything quiet now made an abrupt turn and we were visited by TV stations and Network News crews including CNN, HBO, and *Entertainment Tonight*. With our cover blown, the decision was made to take advantage of the publicity. Besides, we knew the *Los Angeles Times* was about to run a major story entitled "Under Surveillance," which would also reveal my concern about the telephone wiretaps I suspected, along with the fact that a letter from another real member of the S.I.S. had been sent to me after he had gotten hold of our screenplay.

As the day progressed, I went through three cellular batteries since, no sooner would I get off one call talking to the Teamsters, than I was on again trying to find out why a multi-million-dollar production couldn't cash checks for a few hundred dollars from its bank account.

When the Jeep stunt was delayed, the production staff started juggling the rest of the day's shots, trying to keep our schedule from falling behind.

The production manager had his hands full, placating vendors who were blowing their tops and trying to calm a frustrated director who was still waiting, after three hours, for the stunt coordinator to get one done. (In the end, if a schedule goes over budget, there's a lot of finger-pointing, but it's usually the director who gets stuck with the blame, no matter who is at fault.)

The incredibly popular location, combined with a huge film company, attracted several thousand beach tourists including . . . a number of local gang members. As I spoke to Tom Hallick, a friend I had invited to the set, I was informed by the location manager that one of the gangs had just threatened to vandalize our set. They were uptight because we had called in an outside graffiti artist to help our production designer finish the background sets. They said this area was theirs and unless we gave them additional space to "tag" with their own graffiti, they would retaliate.

Juggling those issues was immediately overshadowed by what happened to Tom. Just after we'd said goodbye, a gang member took a shot at him as he had gotten into his car. The bullet took out the front wind-shield of his new Cadillac and narrowly missed his head. He was so incensed that he started chasing the kid with the gun, until he realized what he was doing. Lucky for him, the gang member disappeared down a nearby alley.

Somewhere in the middle of all this, the production accountant telephoned me to say he didn't have any money, again. It was a call that put me right over the top. I'm sure that I seemed crazed to others as I stood in the middle of the street screaming into the phone. I'd had it with excuses and knew he wasn't telling the truth about what was happening. I listened to his last excuse and hung up on him. (Within another week he was fired.)

I immediately called the bond company and pleaded for their help. Within an hour I had a leather bag with ten thousand in cash delivered to the set to calm down the street vendors and take care of our other immediate needs. Shortly thereafter, we got a complicated series of stunt shots off, but told the stunt coordinator his services, too, were terminated. He was replaced the next morning.

The graffiti gang, meanwhile, had been given new walls to cover and was busy re-doing the background scenery.

In between, I called the Teamsters two more times and the labor lawyer. The Teamsters granted one more day of grace and were willing to keep talking.

When the news and TV crews from CNN and *Entertainment Tonight* showed up, the atmosphere took on a carnival setting. Between us there were seven cameras on the set. While our P.R. company tried to make sure the reporters were satisfied with their interviews and shots, the production manager and director picked up speed and got us back on schedule. Within hours, CNN was broadcasting a series of pieces on us across the country, while HBO satellite fed its video report worldwide about the making of the movie. *Entertainment Tonight* put together its own five-minute piece on "S.I.S." and made it the lead-in story seen by thirty million television viewers a few nights later. Even *Newsweek* picked up the story that week.

Now, at last, with the last day of shooting approaching, I thought we'd seen it all. I was wrong.

THE LAST SHOT

On the final day of shooting, I drove through the Antelope Valley toward the house we had chosen as Scott Glenn's home in the movie. Remarkably, we had gone only one day over schedule and added an additional day on our own for a total of twenty-seven days of principal photography. And although we had filmed quite a few action sequences, that last day's schedule called for a major confrontation between Lou Diamond Phillips and Scott Glenn. Their fight had been planned and choreographed days in advance by our new stunt coordinator, Bobby Foxworth.

The war between them would take the full day to shoot. It would begin in the house's living room, crash into the den, blow through the French glass door and into the kitchen. Then it would explode out through a large picture window into the front yard. From there, Bobby set up a series of cuts that sent both stars through two balsa-wood fences and finally into a corral. It was a hellova brawl, as anyone who has seen the movie will attest. It went relatively smoothly until we got to the part where the stunt men went through the four-by-five-foot window.

Multiple cameras covered the shot from both inside the house and out in the front yard. Holding on to each other, the two men spun like a top, flinging themselves through the window and crash-landed in the yard. When they both stood up, each stunt man was cut; one of them had a broken wrist. The other found a half inch piece of glass buried in his hand. (I don't care what anybody says, regardless of preparation and years of experience of the stunt people involved, all stunts carry the risk of injury.)

We had both men rushed to the hospital. The shot was nearly complete and we figured out a way to bypass the last part of it. What truly amazed me was to see both of these guys back on the set less than ninety minutes later, asking for a chance to finish their work! As far as I'm concerned, stunt men and women are a breed apart from the rest of us.

As the last scene of the movie was set up, I will never forget how I felt. It had taken four tough years to get there, and then only twenty-seven days to shoot the film. Even though the post-production process would last another five months, these last few minutes were the emotional ones for me.

Through all the years and trips to the AFM and Cannes, and thousands of phone calls and hundreds of meetings, and through countless rewrites, one thing had remained pretty much intact: the last few lines of dialogue on the last page of the script. Now, watching Scott Glenn bring the words on the page to life was a moment I had always envisioned, a moment I didn't want to end.

When it was over, I stood away, looking on as the cast and crew said goodbye. I was thinking of our many shared experiences. They were the kinds of experiences only movies can invoke.

And, to the cast and crew who made
it all happen . . .
you have my thanks
for making it a once-in-a-lifetime experience for me.

APPENDIX

The Research Department is a fee-based information
brokerage located in Tarzana, California. Since 1986
they have provided computer-assisted research
support services primarily to the entertainment
community. With instant access to thousands of
magazines and newspapers from around the world,
this unique research company is often the first place
that television and film producers turn for
background information on a wide range of
conventional and unconventional subjects. The
Research Department provided the following S.I.S.-
related headlines and dates and may be contacted at
818-342-5355 by any person interested in locating
additional information.

STORY LEADS FROM THE
LOS ANGELES TIMES

Heading #1
FBI INVESTIGATION SHUTS ROAD
Los Angeles Times - SUNDAY November 15, 1992

Heading #2
JURY TO DECIDE SUIT AGAINST L.A. IN MCDONALD'S HEIST
Los Angeles Times - SATURDAY October 10, 1992

Heading #3
FAMILY'S SUIT BLAMES POLICE IN VAN NUYS MAN'S DEATH
Los Angeles Times - THURSDAY September 24, 1992

Heading #4
FAMILY OF SLAIN MAN SUES POLICE COURTS: CIVIL RIGHTS FILING ALLEGES THAT UNDERCOVER OFFICERS WATCHED AS HE WAS FATALLY SHOT OUTSIDE A NORTH HILLS MCDONALD'S, WHICH IS ALSO NAMED AS A DEFENDANT.
Los Angeles Times - THURSDAY September 24, 1992

Heading #5
3 SUSPECTS LEAD POLICE ON 20-MINUTE STREET CHASE CRIME: A CAR SPOTTED IN CHATSWORTH AFTER A ROBBERY FLEES TO VALLEY VILLAGE. TWO PATROL CARS CRASH AND THE THREE ARE EVENTUALLY ARRESTED.
Los Angeles Times - FRIDAY September 18, 1992

Heading #6
L.A. APPROVES ATTORNEY'S FEE IN POLICE BRUTALITY SUIT
Los Angeles Times - WEDNESDAY August 12, 1992

Heading #7
COUNCIL AGREES TO PAY LEGAL FEES IN BRUTALITY SUIT
Los Angeles Times - WEDNESDAY August 12, 1992

Heading #8
UNDER SURVEILLANCE?
'S.I.S' PRODUCERS WONDER IF LAPD UNIT IS FOCUSING ON THEM
Los Angeles Times - MONDAY August 10, 1992

Heading #9
CITY WON'T APPEAL AWARD TO ATTORNEYS
Los Angeles Times - SATURDAY August 8, 1992

Heading #10
ATTORNEYS AWARDED FEE OF $378,000 IN BRUTALITY SUIT
Los Angeles Times - WEDNESDAY August 5, 1992

Heading #11
VOTING PRACTICES COULD BE KEY TO COUNCIL LIABILITY
COURTS: A JUDGE REFUSES TO DROP LAWMAKERS AS
DEFENDANTS IN A $20-MILLION BRUTALITY SUIT
AGAINST THE LAPD. SCHOLARS CALL THE RULING
GROUNDBREAKING.
Los Angeles Times - SATURDAY August 1, 1992

Heading #12
4 LAWSUITS OVER POLICE ACTIONS SETTLED
LAPD: COUNCIL AGREES TO PAY A TOTAL OF $1.6
MILLION. ONE INCIDENT INVOLVES THE SLAYING OF A
SUSPECT BY A MEMBER OF THE
SPECIAL INVESTIGATIONS SECTION.
Los Angeles Times - FRIDAY July 31, 1992

Frank Sacks

Heading #13
COUNCIL LOSS OF IMMUNITY IN BRUTALITY CASE
APPEALED
Los Angeles Times - FRIDAY July 24, 1992

Heading #14
RULING REMOVING COUNCIL IMMUNITY TO BE
APPEALED
Los Angeles Times - FRIDAY July 24, 1992

Heading #15
CITY COUNCIL FACES TRIAL IN BRUTALITY CASE
COURTS: A JUDGE RULES THE OFFICIALS CAN BE HELD
LIABLE IN A $20-MILLION SUIT OVER THE 1990
POLICE SLAYING OF THREE ROBBERS IN SUNLAND.
Los Angeles Times - WEDNESDAY July 22, 1992

Heading #16
MEMBERS OF COUNCIL MAY FACE TRIAL IN POLICE SUIT
COURTS: A JUDGE RULES THAT THEY COULD BE HELD
PERSONALLY LIABLE FOR DAMAGES IN A BRUTALITY
CASE BECAUSE THEY VOTED TO PAY AN EARLIER
JUDGMENT AGAINST THE FORMER CHIEF AND OTHER
OFFICERS.
Los Angeles Times - WEDNESDAY July 22, 1992

Heading #17
MAN SENTENCED FOR ROBBING WOMAN
Los Angeles Times - WEDNESDAY July 15, 1992

Heading #18
SUSPECTED 'PILLOWCASE BANDITS' SEIZED AT BANK
Los Angeles Times - TUESDAY June 30, 1992

Heading #19
'FOLLOW HOME' ROBBER PLEADS GUILTY
CRIME: THE MAN WILL BE SENTENCED JULY 14 FOR HIS
ROLE IN THE WOODLAND HILLS INCIDENT. TWO
CO-DEFENDANTS WILL HAVE HEARINGS THURSDAY.
Los Angeles Times - TUESDAY June 16, 1992

Heading #20
LAWYER CRITICIZES L.A. VOTE TO PAY POLICE DAMAGES
LAWSUITS: STEPHEN YAGMAN SAYS COUNCIL MEMBERS
THEMSELVES CAN NOW BE HELD LIABLE IN THE
CASE, WHICH INVOLVED THE 1990 KILLING OF
THREE ROBBERS IN SUNLAND.
Los Angeles Times - FRIDAY May 29, 1992

Heading #21
FOUR FACE CHARGES IN FOLLOW-HOME ROBBERY CASE
Los Angeles Times - FRIDAY May 29, 1992

Heading #22
VICTIMS CAREFULLY CHOSEN, POLICE SAY
WOODLAND HILLS: INVESTIGATORS BELIEVE FOUR
PEOPLE IN CUSTODY ARE PART OF A LARGER RING THAT
COMMITS THE SOPHISTICATED 'FOLLOW-HOME'
ROBBERIES.
Los Angeles Times - THURSDAY May 28, 1992

Heading #23
FOUR FACE CHARGES IN FOLLOW-HOME ROBBERY CASE
Los Angeles Times - THURSDAY May 28, 1992

Heading #24
CITY, NOT GATES, WILL PAY SUIT DAMAGES
EXCESSIVE FORCE: JURY HAD WANTED CHIEF AND
OFFICERS INVOLVED TO FOOT $44,000 BILL THEMSELVES.
Los Angeles Times - THURSDAY May 28, 1992

Heading #25
AUTHORITIES ARREST 4 AFTER 'FOLLOW-HOME' ROBBERY
CRIME: OFFICERS OF A CONTROVERSIAL UNIT TRAILED
ONE SUSPECT FOR THREE WEEKS. A WOODLAND
HILLS WOMAN IS THE VICTIM IN THE LATEST HOLDUP.
Los Angeles Times - WEDNESDAY May 27, 1992

Heading #26
'FOLLOW-HOME' ROBBERY SUSPECTS ARRESTED
Los Angeles Times - WEDNESDAY May 27, 1992

Heading #27
VERDICT AGAINST SIS OFFICERS
Los Angeles Times - SUNDAY April 26, 1992

Heading #28
LAWYER BILLS L.A. $987,684 IN POLICE SUIT
COURTS: THE ATTORNEY WON $44,000 AWARD AGAINST
CHIEF DARYL F. GATES AND THE OFFICERS WHO
SHOT FOUR ROBBERS, KILLING THREE.
Los Angeles Times - THURSDAY April 9, 1992

Heading #29
LAWYER BILLS CITY IN POLICE SUIT: $987,684
CIVIL RIGHTS: HE WON A $44,000 JURY AWARD FOR HIS
CLIENTS AGAINST CHIEF DARYL F. GATES AND
SEVERAL OFFICERS. THE FEE BROUGHT IMMEDIATE
CRITICISM.
Los Angeles Times - THURSDAY April 9, 1992

Heading #30
JURY DECISION IN ROBBERS' DEATHS
Los Angeles Times - THURSDAY April 9, 1992

Heading #31
INVESTIGATOR OF OFFICERS FACES THE GLARE OF
SCRUTINY
Los Angeles Times - TUESDAY April 7, 1992

Heading #32
ATTORNEY RESCINDS OFFER TO DROP COUNCIL SUIT
Los Angeles Times - FRIDAY April 3, 1992

Heading #33
LAWYER WITHDRAWS OFFER TO DROP COUNCIL FROM
SUIT
Los Angeles Times - FRIDAY April 3, 1992

Heading #34
COUNCIL SUED OVER FATAL POLICE SHOOTING
LAPD: ATTORNEY OFFERS TO DROP MEMBERS AS
DEFENDANTS IF THEY MAKE GATES PAY DAMAGES
ASSESSED IN SAME INCIDENT. OFFICIALS ANGRILY
CHARGE EXTORTION.
Los Angeles Times - THURSDAY April 2, 1992

Heading #35
GATES SHOULD PAY SIS SUIT DAMAGES,
3 ON COUNCIL SAY
COURTS: YAROSLAVSKY, RIDLEY-THOMAS AND
GALANTER WANT TO FOLLOW JURY'S WISHES THAT NO
TAXPAYER MONEY BE USED IN PENALTIES FOR POLICE
SLAYING OF THREE ROBBERS.
Los Angeles Times - WEDNESDAY April 1, 1992

Heading #36
3 ON COUNCIL WANT GATES TO PAY LAWSUIT DAMAGES
Los Angeles Times - WEDNESDAY April 1, 1992

Heading #37
GATES, SPECIAL UNIT FOUND LIABLE FOR ROBBERS'
DEATHS
Los Angeles Times - TUESDAY March 31, 1992

Heading #38
GATES WANTS TO BE 'JUDGE, JURY, EXECUTIONER,'
LAWYER SAYS
Los Angeles Times - WEDNESDAY March 25, 1992

Heading #39
GATES DEFENDS METHOD OF QUESTIONING OFFICERS
Los Angeles Times - WEDNESDAY March 18, 1992

Heading #40
GATES DEFENDS WORK OF SURVEILLANCE UNIT
Los Angeles Times - SATURDAY March 14, 1992

Heading #41
OFFICER TESTIFIES IN SUIT OVER MCDONALD'S KILLINGS
Los Angeles Times - THURSDAY March 5, 1992

Heading #42
L.A. DETECTIVE TELLS DETAILS OF FATAL SHOOTING
CIVIL RIGHTS: THE OFFICER IS TESTIFYING IN FEDERAL
COURT AS A DEFENDANT IN A SUIT ALLEGING THE
SPECIAL INVESTIGATIONS SECTION KILLED THREE
UNARMED ROBBERS.
Los Angeles Times - THURSDAY March 5, 1992

Heading #43
RULING FAVORING ELITE LAPD UNIT IS UPHELD
Los Angeles Times - TUESDAY March 3, 1992

Heading #44
POLICE NEVER MOVED TO STOP ROBBERY, WOMAN
TESTIFIES
CRIME: ONLY AFTER HOLDUP DID SHE LEARN THEY HAD
BEEN WAITING OUTSIDE RESTAURANT, SHE SAYS. THREE
OF THE FOUR ROBBERS WERE KILLED BY OFFICERS, WHO
ARE NOW BEING SUED.
Los Angeles Times - WEDNESDAY February 26, 1992

Heading #45
CHRISTOPHER REPORT CAN BE USED IN SUIT AGAINST
POLICE
COURTS: A SPECIAL PANEL'S FINDINGS ON THE LAPD ARE
RULED RELEVANT IN THE CASE INVOLVING THE
SHOOTING OF FOUR ROBBERS.
Los Angeles Times - FRIDAY February 21, 1992

Heading #46
ORDER FINDING FBI AGENT IN CONTEMPT OF COURT
REVERSED
Los Angeles Times - WEDNESDAY February 19, 1992

Heading #47
CHRISTOPHER REPORT: IT CUTS BOTH WAYS
COURTS: THE FINDINGS OF THE CITY-COMMISSIONED
PANEL COULD WORK AGAINST L.A. WHEN JURORS
RULE IN POLICE BRUTALITY SUITS.
Los Angeles Times - TUESDAY February 4, 1992

Heading #48
FBI AGENT IS ORDERED JAILED, FREED BY JUDGE
COURTS: ACTION IS DESIGNED TO SPEED APPEAL OF
CONTEMPT ORDER ISSUED FOR HIS REFUSAL TO TESTIFY
IN CIVIL SUIT OVER LAPD SHOOTING.
Los Angeles Times - FRIDAY January 31, 1992

Frank Sacks

Heading #49
FBI AGENT IS FREE DESPITE JAIL ORDER
COURTS: THE DECREE IS INTENDED TO SPEED AN APPEAL
OF A CONTEMPT RULING AGAINST RICHARD
BOEH, WHO IS INVESTIGATING A POLICE SHOOTING.
Los Angeles Times - FRIDAY January 31, 1992

Heading #50
U.S. APPEAL OF CONTEMPT ORDER FAILS
COURTS: THE REQUEST IS DENIED BECAUSE THE CITED FBI
AGENT REMAINS UNPUNISHED. HE REFUSED
TO TESTIFY IN A TRIAL INVOLVING THE SLAYING OF
THREE ROBBERS.
Los Angeles Times - THURSDAY January 30, 1992

Heading #51
METRO DIGEST / LOCAL NEWS IN BRIEF
U.S. JUSTICE DEPT. APPEAL DENIED ON TECHNICALITY
Los Angeles Times - THURSDAY January 30, 1992

Heading #52
METRO DIGEST / LOCAL NEWS IN BRIEF
U.S. TO APPEAL CONTEMPT ORDER AGAINST FBI AGENT
Los Angeles Times - SATURDAY January 25, 1992

Heading #53
FBI AGENT IS HELD IN CONTEMPT
COURTS: HE REFUSES TO TESTIFY, UNDER DIRECTION OF
JUSTICE DEPARTMENT ATTORNEYS, ABOUT A
FEDERAL INQUIRY INTO AN L.A. POLICE SPECIAL
INVESTIGATION SECTION SHOOTING.
Los Angeles Times - FRIDAY January 24, 1992

Heading #54
BRADLEY DIFFERS WITH GATES ON PANEL REPORT BUT
BACKS POLICE UNIT
Los Angeles Times - SATURDAY January 18, 1992

Heading #55
BRADLEY CITES PROBLEMS OF EXCESSIVE FORCE BY LAPD
COURTS: HE CONTRADICTS CHIEF GATES AT TRIAL
INVOLVING DEATHS OF THREE ROBBERY SUSPECTS, BUT
MAYOR ALSO DEFENDS SPECIAL INVESTIGATION SECTION
AS LEGITIMATE.
Los Angeles Times - SATURDAY January 18, 1992

Heading #56
GATES DEFENDS HIMSELF, LAPD UNIT AT TRIAL
POLICE: CHIEF SAYS INSTANCES OF EXCESSIVE FORCE OR
RACISM BY OFFICERS ARE RARE. CIVIL SUIT
ACCUSES SPECIAL TEAM OF NEEDLESSLY KILLING THREE
SUSPECTS.
Los Angeles Times - FRIDAY January 17, 1992

Heading #57
GATES SEES NO PATTERN OF EXCESSIVE FORCE OR RACISM
POLICE: THE CHIEF DEFENDS THE DEPARTMENT IN A
TRIAL OVER A FATAL SHOOTING IN 1990. HE IS
ASKED FEW QUESTIONS ABOUT A SURVEILLANCE UNIT.
Los Angeles Times - FRIDAY January 17, 1992

Heading #58
FBI PROBES SLAYING OF ROBBERS BY LAPD
POLICE: EXISTENCE OF INQUIRY CAME TO LIGHT IN SUIT
OVER SIS UNIT'S KILLINGS OF THREE MEN WHO
HAD ROBBED A VALLEY RESTAURANT.
Los Angeles Times - THURSDAY January 16, 1992

Heading #59
SIS SQUAD DESCRIBES SHOOTINGS
COURTS: ROBBERS WERE SHOT AFTER THEY BRANDISHED
GUNS, DETECTIVES TESTIFY. THE THE SURVIVING
VICTIM HAS SAID THAT HE AND HIS ACCOMPLICES WERE
UNARMED.
Los Angeles Times - WEDNESDAY January 15, 1992

Heading #60
VICTIMS' SUIT TARGETS TACTICS OF POLICE UNIT IN '90
KILLINGS
Los Angeles Times - FRIDAY January 10, 1992

Heading #61
ATTORNEY CALLS SPECIAL LAPD SQUAD 'ASSASSINS' AS
CIVIL RIGHTS TRIAL OPENS
COURTS: CASE WILL FOCUS ON TACTICS OF SPECIAL
INVESTIGATIONS OFFICERS WHO FATALLY SHOT THREE
ROBBERS.
Los Angeles Times - FRIDAY January 10, 1992

Heading #62
PROFILE / MARK A. KROEKER
MAKING BELIEVERS OUT OF THE SKEPTICS
POLICE: THE ASSISTANT CHIEF IS ONE OF 32 CANDIDATES
SEEKING DARYL GATES' JOB.
Los Angeles Times - SUNDAY December 22, 1991

Heading #63
BOY WHO WAS FETUS WHEN FATHER DIED IS ALLOWED
TO SUE
LAW: COURT SAYS CHILD HAS RIGHT TO CLAIM HE WAS
DEPRIVED OF CIVIL RIGHTS BY 1982 KILLING AT
HANDS OF LAPD UNIT.
Los Angeles Times - TUESDAY November 5, 1991

Heading #64
FEDERAL JUDGE WON'T ORDER CHRISTOPHER TO TESTIFY
IN CIVIL SUIT
COURTS: BUT THE JURIST SAYS HE WOULD BE WELCOMED
AS A VOLUNTARY WITNESS IN THE TRIAL OF 22
POLICE OFFICERS ACCUSED OF VIOLATING THE RIGHTS OF
THREE ROBBERS.
Los Angeles Times - WEDNESDAY October 9, 1991

Heading #65
CAN CHRISTOPHER TESTIFY IN BRUTALITY CASES?
COURTS: HE IS SUBPOENAED TO APPEAR AS A WITNESS
BECAUSE OF HIS ROLE ON COMMISSION. BATTLE
LOOMS OVER WHETHER HE IS AN LAPD 'EXPERT' OR
WHETHER HE IS JUST AWARE OF HEARSAY.
Los Angeles Times - SUNDAY September 29, 1991

Heading #66
JUDGE CRITICIZES CITY ATTORNEY'S OFFICE FOR DELAYS
IN PRETRIAL PROCEEDINGS
COURT: JURIST SAYS HAHN'S ASSISTANT HAS MADE A
'MESS' OUT OF THE CASE SO FAR. LAWYER CLAIMS SUCH
TACTICS ARE COMMON IN POLICE MISCONDUCT CASES.
Los Angeles Times - SATURDAY August 31, 1991

Heading #67
DOG KILLING BY EX-OFFICER PROBED
Los Angeles Times - SATURDAY August 24, 1991

Heading #68
BACKGROUND OF THE SIS
Los Angeles Times - FRIDAY August 16, 1991

Heading #69
MAN RUN DOWN BY POLICE CAR WINS $890,000
Los Angeles Times - FRIDAY August 16, 1991

Heading #70
METRO DIGEST / LOCAL NEWS IN BRIEF
7 TOLD TO EXPLAIN ABSENCE AT DEPOSITIONS IN SIS SUIT
Los Angeles Times - THURSDAY June 27, 1991

Heading #71
PERSPECTIVES ON POLICE
LAPD: CONFIDENT IN BRUTALITY THE INDEPENDENCE
THAT SALVAGED THE DEPARTMENT FROM CORRUPTION
NOW CAUSES ITS TROUBLES. THE CURE IS
ACCOUNTABILITY.
Los Angeles Times - THURSDAY March 21, 1991

Heading #72
THE CANDIDATES RESPOND
Los Angeles Times - SUNDAY January 20, 1991

Heading #73
THE CANDIDATES RESPOND
Los Angeles Times - SUNDAY January 20, 1991

Heading #74
SUIT SAYS LAPD WAS NEGLIGENT
LITIGATION: A WOMAN SEEKS $1 MILLION AFTER SHE
WAS ROBBED AT A SUNLAND MCDONALD'S WHILE
OFFICERS STAKING OUT THE RESTAURANT FAILED TO
STOP THE CRIME.
Los Angeles Times - FRIDAY August 3, 1990

Heading #75
MAN SENTENCED IN ROBBERIES OF MCDONALD'S
Los Angeles Times - WEDNESDAY July 25, 1990

Heading #76
ROBBER WHO SURVIVED SHOOT-OUT THAT KILLED
3 ACCOMPLICES IS JAILED 17 YEARS
Los Angeles Times - WEDNESDAY July 25, 1990

Heading #77
MAN ADMITS FAST-FOOD HOLDUPS IN EXCHANGE FOR
LESSER SENTENCE
Los Angeles Times - SATURDAY June 16, 1990

Heading #78
METRO DIGEST / LOCAL NEWS IN BRIEF
SHOOT-OUT SURVIVOR PLEADS GUILTY TO ROBBERY
Los Angeles Times - SATURDAY June 16, 1990

Heading #79
POLICE RESCUE TWO KIDNAPED WOMEN HELD FOR
RANSOM
Los Angeles Times - TUESDAY June 12, 1990

Heading #80
'ROBBER'S RIGHTS' CASE GOES TO JURY
TRIAL: WOMAN SAYS POLICE SURVEILLANCE SQUAD
VIOLATED HER CIVIL RIGHTS IN SHOOTING. OFFICERS SAY
THEY WERE JUST DOING THEIR JOB.
Los Angeles Times - FRIDAY June 8, 1990

Heading #81
6 SIS DETECTIVES CLEARED IN SHOOTING OF BANK
ROBBERS
Los Angeles Times - FRIDAY June 8, 1990

Heading #82
METRO DIGEST / LOCAL NEWS IN BRIEF
SIS OFFICERS JUSTIFIED IN SHOOTING, COURT TOLD
Los Angeles Times - THURSDAY June 7, 1990

Heading #83
L.A. DETECTIVE IN SECRET UNIT DEFENDS KILLING BANK
ROBBER
Los Angeles Times - WEDNESDAY June 6, 1990

Heading #84
SIS OFFICERS ACCUSED IN $10-MILLION CIVIL SUIT
POLICE: 6 RETIRED AND CURRENT MEMBERS OF
CONTROVERSIAL SQUAD ARE ACCUSED OF VIOLATING
RIGHTS OF 2 BANK ROBBERS BY WOUNDING ONE AND
KILLING THE OTHER, WHO WAS UNARMED.
Los Angeles Times - MONDAY June 4, 1990

Heading #85
DEFENSE LOSES--MURDER CASE DISMISSED
Los Angeles Times - WEDNESDAY May 30, 1990

Heading #86
MURDER CASE IS DISMISSED OVER DEFENSE'S OPPOSITION
COURTS: A PUBLIC DEFENDER WANTS HIS CLIENT
PROSECUTED FOR THREE KILLINGS TO FORCE THE
DISCLOSURE OF POLICE FILES.
Los Angeles Times - WEDNESDAY May 30, 1990

Heading #87
D.A. WANTS MURDER CASE DROPPED BUT DEFENSE
OBJECTS
Los Angeles Times - SATURDAY May 26, 1990

Heading #88
D.A. TRIES TO DROP CHARGES BUT DEFENSE IS HESITANT
HEARINGS: ALFREDO OLIVAS IS ACCUSED OF MURDER
AFTER A POLICE SHOOT-OUT IN WHICH THREE MEN
DIED. PROSECUTORS ARE UNCERTAIN THEY COULD
PROVE HE PROVOKED THE SHOOTING.
Los Angeles Times - SATURDAY May 26, 1990

Heading #89
3 SUSPECTS IN KIDNAP CAUGHT ON OLVERA ST.
CRIME: VICTIM ESCAPED AFTER THREE MEN WHO
APPROACHED SISTER CARRYING RANSOM WERE
ARRESTED IN POPULAR TOURIST SPOT. A FOURTH MAN
WAS CAPTURED LATER AT ANOTHER LOCATION.
Los Angeles Times - SUNDAY April 15, 1990

Heading #90
DIGEST / LOCAL NEWS IN BRIEF
JUDGE IN MURDER TRIAL ORDERS SIS RECORDS
Los Angeles Times - THURSDAY March 22, 1990

Heading #91
POLICE SHOOTINGS IN LOS ANGELES
Los Angeles Times - TUESDAY February 27, 1990

Heading #92
LONE SURVIVOR IN SHOOT-OUT CHARGED
WITH 3 MURDERS
Los Angeles Times - WEDNESDAY February 28, 1990

Heading #93
SAFER STREETS ARE PRICELESS: LESS-PAINFUL
ENFORCEMENT WOULD BE, TOO
POLICE: L.A.'S FORCE MAY KEEP US BETTER PROTECTED
THAN NEW YORKERS, BUT THERE'S A PRICE IN CIVILIZED
BEHAVIOR.
Los Angeles Times - MONDAY February 26, 1990

Heading #94
METRO DIGEST LOCAL NEWS IN BRIEF
FAMILIES OF SUSPECTS IN HOLDUP SUE FOR $10 MILLION
Los Angeles Times - THURSDAY February 22, 1990

Heading #95
SUIT FILED BY RELATIVES OF MEN SLAIN BY POLICE
MCDONALD'S HOLDUP: A $10-MILLION ACTION SAYS THE
SPECIAL INVESTIGATIONS SECTION'S MISSION IS
TO EXECUTE CRIMINAL SUSPECTS.
Los Angeles Times - THURSDAY February 22, 1990

Heading #96
$10-MILLION LAWSUIT FILED IN
SLAYINGS AT MCDONALD'S
Los Angeles Times - THURSDAY February 22, 1990

Heading #97
ROBBER A VICTIM, WIFE SAYS
FAMILY AT A LOSS TO EXPLAIN CRIME ROLE
Los Angeles Times - MONDAY February 19, 1990

Heading #98
MAN CHARGED WITH MURDER IN ROBBERY
Los Angeles Times - THURSDAY February 15, 1990

Heading #99
SLAIN MEN SUSPECTED IN CRIME SPREE
Los Angeles Times - WEDNESDAY February 14, 1990

Heading #100
POLICE SURVEILLANCE UNIT KILLS 3 ROBBERY SUSPECTS
Los Angeles Times - TUESDAY February 13, 1990

Heading #101
METRO DIGEST / LOCAL NEWS IN BRIEF
CONVICTED ROBBER SUES POLICE FOR SHOOTING
Los Angeles Times - SATURDAY December 23, 1989

Heading #102
BOY'S SUIT OVER SLAYING IS DISMISSED
CIVIL RIGHTS: THE CHILD WAS UNBORN WHEN POLICE
KILLED HIS BANK-ROBBER FATHER AND WOUNDED
HIS MOTHER. THEREFORE, HE HAS NO LEGAL STANDING
TO SUE, A JUDGE RULES.
Los Angeles Times - TUESDAY December 5, 1989

Heading #103
LAPD UNIT A DEATH SQUAD, SUIT ALLEGES
SON OF MAN KILLED BY POLICE CLAIMS CIVIL RIGHTS
WERE VIOLATED
Los Angeles Times - TUESDAY September 12, 1989

Heading #104
6 CHARGED IN $70,000 WELFARE FRAUD CASE
Los Angeles Times - SATURDAY April 15, 1989

Heading #105
ONLY IN L.A. / PEOPLE AND EVENTS
Los Angeles Times - TUESDAY April 4, 1989

Heading #106
SIS OFFICER WOUNDS SUSPECT AFTER BEING STRUCK
BY CAR
Los Angeles Times - WEDNESDAY March 29, 1989

Heading #107
METRO DIGEST
LOCAL NEWS IN BRIEF
OFFICER SHOOTS DRIVER AFTER BEING HIT
Los Angeles Times - WEDNESDAY March 29, 1989

Heading #108
OFFICER HIT BY CAR
POLICE SHOOT SUSPECT IN AUTO THEFT
Los Angeles Times - WEDNESDAY March 29, 1989

Heading #109
POLICE DEFEND ACTIONS IN KIDNAPING, CITING FEAR
FOR VICTIMS' LIVES
Los Angeles Times - FRIDAY March 17, 1989

Heading #110
QUESTIONS REMAIN AFTER KIDNAPING SUSPECT SHOT
Los Angeles Times - THURSDAY March 16, 1989Heading

Heading #111
TO PROTECT AND TO SERVE
Los Angeles Times - THURSDAY February 16, 1989

Heading #112
UNDERCOVER POLICE TOLD TO PROTECT PUBLIC FIRST
NEW POLICY IS RESPONSE TO REPORTS OF FAILURE TO
INTERVENE BY SURVEILLANCE UNIT DURING CRIMES
Los Angeles Times - TUESDAY February 14, 1989

Heading #113
IN RETROSPECT 1988
FIRES, GUNFIRE – AND A FEW CHEERS – PUNCTUATE THE
YEAR FOR LOS ANGELES
Los Angeles Times - SATURDAY December 31, 1988

 Heading #114
GATES STRONGLY DEFENDS SIS, SAYS MATTER
IS CLOSED
Los Angeles Times - THURSDAY November 3, 1988

Heading #115
DIED ON ANTI-DRUG MISSION
TWO KILLED IN COPTER CRASH EULOGIZED
Los Angeles Times - SUNDAY October 30, 1988

Heading #116
POLICE SUED OVER SPECIAL UNIT'S SHOOTING
OF ROBBERS
Los Angeles Times - TUESDAY October 25, 1988

Heading #117
SUIT HITS POLICE 'DEATH SQUAD'
Los Angeles Times - MONDAY October 24, 1988
STORY TYPE: WIRE

Heading #118
LAPD'S SECRETIVE INVESTIGATIONS UNIT: WATCHING AS
SUSPECTS COMMIT CRIMES
Los Angeles Times - SATURDAY October 8, 1988

Heading #119
COUNCIL ORDERS GATES TO EXPLAIN UNIT'S MISSION
Los Angeles Times - WEDNESDAY October 5, 1988

STORY LEADS FROM
THE LOS ANGELES DAILY NEWS

Heading #1
RESTAURANT WORKER CLEARED TO SUE POLICE OVER
ROBBERY
Los Angeles Daily News - SATURDAY December 12, 1992

Heading #2
SAN FERNANDO VALLEY BRIEFLY RULING ALLOWS SUIT
AGAINST POLICE
Los Angeles Daily News - SATURDAY December 12, 1992

Heading #3
JUDGE RULES POLICE-INACTION LAWSUIT
SHOULD GO TO JURY
Los Angeles Daily News - SATURDAY October 10, 1992

Heading #4
L.A. TO PAY LEGAL FEES FOR OFFICERS IN SLAYINGS
Los Angeles Daily News - WEDNESDAY August 12, 1992

Heading #5
GATES, SIS OFFICERS ORDERED TO PAY LAWYERS $378,175
IN BRUTALITY CASE
Los Angeles Daily News - WEDNESDAY August 5, 1992

Heading #6
JUDGE WON'T DROP COUNCIL MEMBERS FROM SUIT OVER
LIABILITY IN SHOOTING
Los Angeles Daily News - SATURDAY August 1, 1992

Heading #7
JUDGE WON'T DROP COUNCIL MEMBERS FROM SUIT OVER
LIABILITY IN SHOOTING
Los Angeles Daily News - SATURDAY August 1, 1992

Heading #8
WILLIAMS REVIEWING SIS, UNITS
Los Angeles Daily News - SATURDAY August 1, 1992

Heading #9
3 BRUTALITY LAWSUITS RESOLVED CITY COUNCIL VOTES
TO PAY $1.2 MILLION
Los Angeles Daily News - THURSDAY July 30, 1992

Heading #10
L.A. OFFICIALS MAY HAVE TO PAY BRUTALITY COSTS
Los Angeles Daily News - WEDNESDAY July 22, 1992

Heading #11
TRIAL ORDERED FOR SUSPECT IN FOLLOW-HOME
ROBBERIES
Los Angeles Daily News - THURSDAY June 25, 1992

Heading #12
'FOLLOW HOME' ROBBERIES DENIED
3 MEN PLEAD NOT GUILTY TO VICTIMIZING UP TO
21 VALLEY WOMEN SINCE MID-1991
Los Angeles Daily News - FRIDAY May 29, 1992

Heading #13
ARRAIGNMENT SET FOR 4 IN FOLLOW-HOME HOLDUP
Los Angeles Daily News - THURSDAY May 28, 1992

Heading #14
4 ROBBERY SUSPECTS ARRESTED MAY BE LINKED TO
STRING OF FOLLOW-HOME CRIMES
Los Angeles Daily News - WEDNESDAY May 27, 1992

Heading #15
ATTORNEYS FIGHT CLAIM INTERVENTION
LAWYERS URGE CITY, COUNTY NOT TO PAY DAMAGES
FOR OFFICERS FINED IN EXCESSIVE-FORCE CASES
Los Angeles Daily News - MONDAY April 13, 1992

Heading #16
OUTSPOKEN ATTORNEY WALKS FINE LINE
CIVIL-RIGHTS DEFENDER HAS SPECIALIZED IN LAPD
EXCESSIVE-FORCE SUITS
Los Angeles Daily News - SUNDAY April 12, 1992

Heading #17
PUBLIC FORUM WILSON TREATS WORKERS AS IF HE
WANTS THEM TO QUIT
Los Angeles Daily News - FRIDAY April 3, 1992

Heading #18
LAWYER TRYING TO MAKE GATES PAY JUDGMENT
Los Angeles Daily News - THURSDAY April 2, 1992

Heading #19
GATES PONDERS DISBANDING SPECIAL UNIT FOUND
LIABLE IN 3 DEATHS
Los Angeles Daily News - WEDNESDAY April 1, 1992

Heading #20
GATES LIABLE IN DEATH
JURY RULES AGAINST CHIEF, 9 OFFICERS
Los Angeles Daily News - TUESDAY March 31, 1992

Heading #21
LAWYER IN SUIT BLASTS GATES, OFFICERS
Los Angeles Daily News - WEDNESDAY March 25,
1992Heading #22

Heading #22
KING'S ATTORNEY IN CIVIL SUIT MONITORING
CRIMINAL TRIAL
Los Angeles Daily News - MONDAY March 23, 1992

Heading #23
GATES IS LAST TO TESTIFY IN SUIT OVER KILLING OF
SUSPECTS
Los Angeles Daily News - THURSDAY March 19, 1992

Heading #24
WITNESS SUPPORTS OFFICERS WHO KILLED
3 ROBBERY SUSPECTS
Los Angeles Daily News - SUNDAY March 15, 1992

Heading #25
GATES DEFENDS OFFICERS WHO KILLED 3 SUSPECTS
Los Angeles Daily News - SATURDAY March 14, 1992

Heading #26
GLENDALE BRIEFLY:
CITY FIRE MARSHAL GETS PROMOTION
Los Angeles Daily News - TUESDAY March 3, 1992

Heading #27
BURBANK BRIEFLY:
KILLING OF ROBBER IS RULED JUSTIFIED
Los Angeles Daily News - TUESDAY March 3, 1992

Heading #28
SAN FERNANDO VALLEY BRIEFLY:
SLAYING WAS JUSTIFIED, APPEALS COURT RULES
Los Angeles Daily News - TUESDAY March 3, 1992

Heading #29
LAPD OFFICER TESTIFIES HE CANCELED 911 CALL
Los Angeles Daily News - THURSDAY February 27, 1992

Heading #30
RESTAURANT MANAGER TESTIFIES THAT POLICE
IGNORED ROBBERY CALL
Los Angeles Daily News - WEDNESDAY February 26,
1992

Heading #31
LAPD POLICY CAN BE WEIGHED IN RIGHTS TRIAL
Los Angeles Daily News - FRIDAY February 21, 1992

Heading #32
FBI AGENT WON'T HAVE TO TESTIFY IN SUIT
Los Angeles Daily News - WEDNESDAY February 19,
1992

Heading #33
COURT MAY MANDATE FBI TESTIMONY
COMMENTS SOUGHT IN SUIT AGAINST OFFICERS
WHO SHOT ROBBERY SUSPECTS
Los Angeles Daily News - SATURDAY February 15, 1992

Heading #34
FBI AGENT ORDERED
ARRESTED JUDGE ACTS TO SPEED APPEAL
IN RIGHTS TRIAL
Los Angeles Daily News - FRIDAY January 31, 1992

Heading #35
U.S. PLANS TO BLOCK TESTIMONY
FBI AGENT ORDER WILL BE APPEALED
Los Angeles Daily News - SATURDAY January 25, 1992

Heading #36
AGENT RULED IN CONTEMPT IN LAPD SHOOTING TRIAL
Los Angeles Daily News - FRIDAY January 24, 1992

Heading #37
$600,000 SETTLEMENT REACHED IN 3RD DALTON AVE.
RAID SUIT
Los Angeles Daily News - THURSDAY January 23, 1992

Heading #38
PLAINTIFF SAYS POLICE DIDN'T TELL HER OF RELATIVES'
DEATHS
Los Angeles Daily News - WEDNESDAY January 22, 1992

Heading #39
BRADLEY DEFENDS LAPD TESTIFIES RACISM, BRUTALITY
EXIST
Los Angeles Daily News - SATURDAY January 18, 1992

Heading #40
GATES REJECTS ABUSE, BIAS CLAIMS CHIEF TESTIFIES IN
LAWSUIT FILED OVER SHOOTINGS
Los Angeles Daily News - FRIDAY January 17, 1992

Heading #41
U.S. SEEKS TO BLOCK TESTIMONY IN SHOOTING BY LAPD
OFFICERS
Los Angeles Daily News - THURSDAY January 16, 1992

Heading #42
ATTORNEY'S LANGUAGE AN ISSUE IN TRIAL
DESCRIPTIONS OF SPECIAL POLICE UNIT ARE CENTER OF
CONTENTION BETWEEN JUDGE, DEFENSE LAWYER
Los Angeles Daily News - SUNDAY January 12, 1992

Heading #43
TRIAL OPENS IN RIGHTS CASE AGAINST OFFICERS,
OFFICIALS
Los Angeles Daily News - FRIDAY January 10, 1992

Heading #44
RULING ALLOWS BOY TO SUE CITY
POLICE KILLED FATHER BEFORE YOUTH'S BIRTH
Los Angeles Daily News - TUESDAY November 5, 1991

Heading #45
HANDLING OF RECORDS CRITICIZED
CITY ATTORNEY ACCUSED OF WITHHOLDING FILES
Los Angeles Daily News - MONDAY October 28, 1991

Heading #46
CHRISTOPHER DOESN'T HAVE TO TESTIFY
HEAD OF PANEL THAT PROBED LAPD
CAN VOLUNTEER TO TAKE STAND IN CIVIL RIGHTS CASE
Los Angeles Daily News - WEDNESDAY October 9, 1991

Heading #47
SHOOTINGS BLAMED ON TOP OFFICIALS
CITY LEADERS CONDONED 'HIT SQUAD', SAYS ATTORNEY
FOR 3 ARMED ROBBERS KILLED BY POLICE
Los Angeles Daily News - MONDAY October 7, 1991

Heading #48
MOTION ON LAPD SUIT TO BE HEARD
JUDGE WILL BE ASKED TO RULE ON LIABILITY OF CITY,
GATES FOR ACTIONS OF SURVEILLANCE UNIT
Los Angeles Daily News - MONDAY September 23, 1991

Heading #49
CITY ATTORNEY, DA KEEPING CASE IN AIR
Los Angeles Daily News - THURSDAY September 12, 1991

Heading #50
6 OFFICERS ACCUSED OF TORTURE, BEATING
Los Angeles Daily News - WEDNESDAY September 11, 1991

Heading #51
EX-POLICE OFFICIALS SCOLDED BY JUDGE FOR
NON-COMPLIANCE
Los Angeles Daily News - SATURDAY August 31, 1991

Heading #52
RETIRED OFFICER COULD FACE CHARGES FOR SHOOTING
DOG
Los Angeles Daily News - SUNDAY August 25, 1991

Heading #53
MAN WINS EXCESSIVE FORCE SUIT CASE AGAINST
DETECTIVE TO COST L.A. $890,000
Los Angeles Daily News - FRIDAY August 16, 1991

Heading #54
SUIT FILED AGAINST LAPD POLICE STOOD BY DURING
ROBBERY, WOMAN SAYS
Los Angeles Daily News - August 4, 1990

Heading #55
MAN SENTENCED FOR ROBBERIES THAT ENDED IN
FATAL SHOOTING OF 3
Los Angeles Daily News - July 25, 1990

Heading #56
DEFENDANT ADMITS ROBBERIES PLEADS GUILTY IN
STRING OF MCDONALD'S HOLDUPS
Los Angeles Daily News - June 16, 1990

Heading #57
SPECIAL POLICE UNIT CLEARED IN '82 SHOOTING OF
ROBBER
Los Angeles Daily News - June 8, 1990

Heading #58
WITNESS CITES 'FOUL-UPS' BY POLICE IN '82 SHOOTOUT
Los Angeles Daily News - June 1, 1990

Heading #59
JUDGE DISMISSES MURDER CHARGES AGAINST
MCDONALD'S ROBBERY SUSPECT
Los Angeles Daily News - May 30, 1990

Heading #60
SPECIAL LAPD UNIT UNDER FIRE ATTORNEY CLAIMS
MEMBERS INDUCED SHOOTOUT WITH CLIENT
Los Angeles Daily News - May 30, 1990

Heading #61
DIMISSAL OF MURDER CHARGE SOUGHT IN SUNLAND
ROBBERY
Los Angeles Daily News - May 26, 1990

Heading #62
SAN FERNANDO VALLEY: BRIEFLY MURDER SUSPECT TO
FACE NEW CHARGES
Los Angeles Daily News - April 19, 1990

Heading #63
ROBBERY SUSPECT PLEADS NOT GUILTY IN KILLINGS
Los Angeles Daily News - February 28, 1990

Heading #64
SURVIVOR FILES LAWSUIT OVER POLICE SHOOTING
Los Angeles Daily News - February 22, 1990

Heading #65
PUBLIC FORUM STOP THE SPRAYING UNTIL MALATHION
FACTS ARE IN
Los Angeles Daily News - February 21, 1990

Heading #66
PUBLIC FORUM SCHOOLS STILL SUFFER FROM
STARVATION FUNDING
Los Angeles Daily News - February 19, 1990

Heading #67
SHOOTING SURVIVOR CHARGED ACCUSED IN DEATHS OF
3 SLAIN BY POLICE
Los Angeles Daily News - February 15, 1990

Heading #68
EDITORIAL PROTECT THE PUBLIC FIRST
Los Angeles Daily News - February 14, 1990

Heading #69
GATES, COMMISSIONER SAY POLICE ACTED PROPERLY IN
SUNLAND SHOOTINGS
Los Angeles Daily News - February 14, 1990

Heading #70
3 SUSPECTS IN ROBBERY ARE SLAIN
POLICE WATCH HOLDUP AT SUNLAND EATERY
Los Angeles Daily News - February 13, 1990

Heading #71
BOY, 7, SUES L.A. OFFICIALS FOR FATHER'S DEATH
Los Angeles Daily News - September 12, 1989

Heading #72
FIVE PLEAD NOT GUILTY IN SIMI DRUG SEIZURE
Los Angeles Daily News - August 25, 1989

Heading #73
OFFICER CHANGES SCENERY
MALIBU STATION HEAD LEAVES URBAN BEAT
Los Angeles Daily News - August 21, 1989

Heading #74
CHATSWORTH POLICE ARREST FOUR TEENS IN 2 STOLEN
CARS
Los Angeles Daily News - March 29, 1989

Heading #75
GATES DEFENDS ACTIONS OF LAPD SPECIAL UNIT
Los Angeles Daily News - November 3, 1988

Heading #76
'DEATH SQUAD' IN LAPD CLAIMED
Los Angeles Daily News - October 25, 1988